James Bartram Nicholson

A Manual of the Art of Bookbinding

James Bartram Nicholson

A Manual of the Art of Bookbinding

ISBN/EAN: 9783742862945

Manufactured in Europe, USA, Canada, Australia, Japa

Cover: Foto ©Thomas Meinert / pixelio.de

Manufactured and distributed by brebook publishing software
(www.brebook.com)

James Bartram Nicholson

A Manual of the Art of Bookbinding

A

MANUAL

OF THE

ART OF BOOKBINDING:

CONTAINING

FULL INSTRUCTIONS IN THE DIFFERENT BRANCHES OF
FORWARDING, GILDING, AND FINISHING.

ALSO,

The Art of Marbling Book-Edges and Paper.

THE WHOLE DESIGNED FOR

THE PRACTICAL WORKMAN, THE AMATEUR, AND THE BOOK-COLLECTOR.

BY

JAMES B. NICHOLSON.

PHILADELPHIA:
HENRY CAREY BAIRD,
INDUSTRIAL PUBLISHER,
406 WALNUT STREET.
1874

PREFACE.

THE progress of the Art of Bookbinding
has made nearly all the works written upon
the subject obsolete; their descriptions no
longer apply to the methods practised by the
best workmen. Throughout this work, the
opinions and remarks of other writers have
been adopted without alteration, unless they
came in contact with practical knowledge.
Every thing that would not bear that test
has been rejected, and in lieu thereof those
modes of operation described that the young
binder will have to learn and practise if he de-
sires to emulate the skill of the best artists.

The plan of the work is taken from
"Arnett's Bibliopegia;" and every thing
given in that work that has any approach
to utility will be found in these pages. It
was at first intended merely to revise that
production; but during the progress of re-
vision so much was rejected that it was

1*   5

deemed better to pass under notice at the same time the labours of others. "Cundall's Ornamental Art" has furnished the early incidents in the "Sketch of the Progress of the Art of Bookbinding;" and, as the best authority upon the subject, "Woolnough's Art of Marbling" has been adapted to this country. Mr. Leighton's "Suggestions in Design" has been laid under contribution in order to enrich the subject of Ornamental Art. The "London Friendly Finishers' Circulars" have been a valuable acquisition to the writer, and it is trusted will make this work equally so to the young finisher. "Cowie's Bookbinders' Manual." "Arnett's School of Design," "Gibb's Handbook of Ornament," and "Scott's Essay on Ornamental Art," in addition to those acknowledged in the body of the work, have supplied some valuable hints.

It is hoped that this volume will prove useful to those forming libraries, by imparting correct information upon subjects that to the book-collector are important, and that its tendencies will be to increase and strengthen a love for the art.   J. B. N.

PHILADELPHIA, 1856.

CONTENTS.

INTRODUCTION.

PART I.

PART II.

PART III.

INTRODUCTION.

SKETCH OF THE PROGRESS OF BOOKBINDING.

THE earliest records of Bookbinding that exist prove that the art has been practised for nearly two thousand years. In past ages, books were written on long scrolls of parchment or papyrus, and were rolled up and fastened with a thong which was made of coloured leather and often highly ornamented. These scrolls were usually attached to one, or, occasionally, two rollers of wood or ivory, or sometimes of gold, much as our large maps are now mounted, and the bosses at the end of the rollers were frequently highly decorated. This decoration may be called the first step toward Ornamental Art applied to the exterior of books.

A learned Athenian, named Phillatius, to whom his countrymen erected a statue, at length found out a means of binding books with glue. The sheets of vellum or papyrus were gathered two or four

9

together, sewn much in the same way as at the
present day; and then, in order to preserve these
sheets, there came, as a matter of course, a covering for the book.

The probability is that the first book-covers were
of wood—plain oaken boards, perhaps; then, as books
in those days were all in manuscript, and very valuable, carved oak bindings were given to those which
were the most decorated within.

To cover the plain wooden board with vellum or
leather would, in the course of years, be too apparent an improvement to be neglected; and specimens
of books so bound, of the great antiquity of which
there are undoubted proofs, exist at the present day.

There is reason to believe that the Romans carried the Art of Binding to considerable perfection.
Some of the public offices had books called Dyptichs,* in which their acts were written. The binding

---

* "The antiquity of illuminated missals has been traced,
conjecturally, even to the time of the apostles themselves.
At the beginning of the Christian era, missive letters were
usually written on tablets of wood, hollowed so as to present
something of the appearance of a boy's slate in a frame.
Two of these were placed face to face to preserve the writing,
which was on wax, and a pair of boards thus prepared was
called a Dyptich. The Epistles of St. Paul and the other

of one of these in carved wood is thus described :—
"Seated in the centre of each board is a consul,
holding in one hand a baton, and in the other, up-
raised, a purse, as if in the act of throwing it to
some victor in the games. Above these are miniature portraits, various other ornaments, and an inscription ; below, on one board, are two men leading
out horses for the race, and beneath them a group,
with a ludicrous representation of two other men,
exhibiting their endurance of pain by allowing crabs
to fasten on their noses." A small print of an
ivory dyptich of the fifth century, in Mr. Arnett's
"Books of the Ancients," may be consulted as a
specimen of the kind of ornament then adopted.

---

apostles to the primitive churches were, in fact, missive
letters despatched to their distant congregations ; and there
is every probability that imaginary or real portraits of the
writers accompanied the letters, and headed the contents
of the Christian dyptichs, in order to insure to them the
same degree of reverence which was paid to the missives
of the government when headed by the imperial effigies.

"The compact form of the dyptich suited the purposes
of a movable altar-piece admirably. And the names
dyptic or triptic, which implied at first but a double or
triple page, came with time to designate those folding altar-
pieces so frequently found in the earliest Christian churches."
—*Lady Calcott's Essay.*

An old writer says, that about the time of the Christian era the books of the Romans were covered with
red, yellow, green, and purple leather, and decorated with gold and silver.

If we pass on to a few centuries later, we find
that the monks were almost the only literati.   They
wrote chiefly on subjects of religion, and bestowed
the greatest pains upon the internal and external
decorations of their books.   In the thirteenth century some of the gospels, missals, and other service-
books for the Greek and Roman churches, were
ornamented with silver and gold, apparently wrought
by the hammer ; sometimes they were enamelled and
enriched with precious stones, and pearls of great
value.   Carved oak figures of the Virgin, or the
Infant Saviour, or of the Crucifixion, were also the
frequent adornments of the outside covers.   One
of these ancient relics is thus described by the
librarian of Henry VIII.

"All I have to do is to observe, that this book
(which the more I have look'd upon the more I
have always admired) hath two thick boards, each
about an inch in thickness, for its covers, and that
they were joined with the book by large leather
thongs, which boards are now by length of time
become very loose.   Tho' I have seen a vast num-

ber of old books and oftentimes examined their
covers, yet I do not remember I ever saw boards
upon any of them of so great thickness as these.
This was the manner of Binding, it seems, of those
times, especially if the books were books of extraordinary value, as this is.   'Twas usual to cut Letters in the Covers, and such letters were the better
preserv'd by having them placed in some hollow
part, which might easily be made if the boards were
pretty thick.   I suppose, therefore, that even the
copies of *Gregory's* Pastoral that were given to
Cathedral Churches by King *Alfred* had such thick
covers also, that these by the *Æstals* might be fix'd
the better.   What makes me think so is, that the
outside of one of the covers of this book is made
hollow, and there is a rude sort of figure upon a
brass plate that is fastened within the hollow part,
which figure I take to have been designed for the
Virgin *Mary*, to whom the Abbey was dedicated.
Over it there was once fastened another much
larger plate, as is plain from the Nails that fixed
it and from some other small indications now ex-
tant,—and this 'tis likely was of silver, and perhaps
there was an *anathema* against the Person that
should presume to alienate it, engraved upon it—
together with the Name of the Person (who it may

2

be was *Roger Poure*) that was the Donor of the
Book. This will make it to have been nothing else
but an Æstal, such a one (tho' not so valuable) as
was fastened upon *Gregory's* Pastoral. But this I
leave to every man's judgment."*

At a later period we find on the binding of books
gold and silver ornaments of very beautiful design,
enclosing precious stones of great variety; carved
ivory tablets let into framework of carved oak;
rich-coloured velvets, edged with morocco, with
bosses, clasps, and corners of solid gold; white vellum stamped in gold and blind tooling; and morocco and calf covers inlaid with various colours
and adorned in every conceivable way. This was
at the end of the fourteenth and in the fifteenth
and sixteenth centuries, when the love of Art was
universal, in the land where Michael Angelo, and
Raffaelle, and Da Vinci produced their great works,
and where, under the auspices of the Medici, the
Art of Bookbinding as well as all other arts was
encouraged.

Mr. Dibdin, in his "Bibliographical Decameron,"
to which we are much indebted, has given an account
of the library of Corvinus, King of Hungary, who

---

* Leland's Itin. vol. ii. p. 86, Oxford, 1769.

died at Buda about the year 1490. This library consisted of about thirty thousand volumes, mostly manuscripts of the Greek and Latin poets and historians, and was contained in large vaulted galleries, in which, among other works of art, were two fountains, one of marble and the other of silver. The binding of the books were mostly of brocade, protected with bosses and clasps of gold and silver; and these, alas! were the subsequent cause of the almost entire destruction of the library; for, when the city of Buda was taken by assault, in 1526, the Turkish soldiers tore the precious volumes from their covers for the sake of the ornaments that were upon them.

The general use of calf and morocco binding seems to have followed the invention of printing. There are many printed books, still in good preservation, that were bound in calf with oaken boards at the end of the fifteenth and beginning of the sixteenth centuries. These are mostly stamped with gold or blind tools. The earliest of these tools generally represent figures, such as Christ, St. Paul, the Virgin, coats of arms, legends, and monograms, according to the contents of the book. Afterward attempts were made to produce pictures, but these were necessarily bad.

In England, the earliest binding with ornament was about the time of Henry VII., when we find the royal arms supported by two angels; the heraldic badge of the double rose and pomegranate, the fleur-de-lys, the portcullis, the emblems of the evangelists, and small ornaments of grotesque animals. There are in the British Museum and in the Record Office many English bindings which undoubtedly were executed in the time of Henry VII.

In the reign of Henry VIII., about 1538, Grafton, the printer, undertook to print the great Bible. Not finding sufficient men or types in England, he went to Paris and there commenced it. He had not, however, proceeded far, before he was stopped in the progress of this heretical book; and he then took over to England the presses, type, printers, and bookbinders, and finished the work in 1539. The edition consisted of 2500 copies, one of which was set up in every church in England, secured to a desk by a chain. Within three years there were seven distinct editions of this work; which, supposing each edition to consist of the same number of copies as the first, would amount to 17,500 folio volumes. The binding, therefore, of so great a number of this book would alone give some importance to the Art of Bookbinding at that period. We

know that Henry VIII. had many splendid volumes
bound in velvet with gold bosses and ornaments. In
his reign the stamping of tools in gold appears to
have been first introduced in England; and some
beautiful rolls, probably from Holbein's designs,
were used as well on the sides as on the gilded edges
of books still in existence.

In the reign of Elizabeth some exquisite bindings
were done in embroidery. The queen herself used
to work covers with gold and silver thread, spangles,
and coloured silk, for Bibles and other devotional
books which she presented to her maids of honour
and her friends. From these brilliant external decorations, many of them entirely inappropriate for a
book, we turn to a purer taste, the exercise of which
will be found to reside within the peculiar limits of
the Bookbinder's Art.

We return to Continental binding, and pass to
the time of the ever-famous Jean Grolier. This
nobleman was the first to introduce lettering upon
the back; and he seems to have taken especial
delight in having the sides of his books ornamented
with very beautiful and elaborate patterns, said to
have been drawn by his own hand. Many of them
exist at the present day, either original Groliers or
copies. Books from his library are eagerly sought
2*

for   All Grolier's books were bound in smooth
morocco or calf, the pattern being formed of intersected line-work, finished by hand with a fine one-
line fillet and gouges to correspond, with the
occasional introduction of a conventional flower.
Sometimes also the patterns were inlaid with morocco of different colours; and it is our opinion that
no style of book-ornamentation has been since introduced that is worthy of entirely superseding the
Grolier, a specimen of which will be given when
treating on style. Very many of the Chevalier's
volumes have the Latin inscription " Johanni Gro-
lierii et amicorum" at the bottom, signifying that
Grolier wished his books to be used by his friends
as well as by himself. Connoisseurs rejoice when
they meet with a work from the library of Maioli,
a disciple of Grolier, or those of Diana of Poictiers,
the mistress of Henry II., and whose books, in
consequence of her influence and taste, are elegantly
bound. It is supposed that the bindings for Diana
of Poictiers were designed by Petit Bernard. They
were bound in morocco of all colours, and usually
ornamented with the emblems of the crescent and
bow and quiver.

     Among the earliest French binders must be men-
tioned Padeloup, Derome, and De Seuil. Pope

celebrates De Seuil in one of his poems. Derome's plain morocco bindings are excellent; they are sewn on raised bands, are firm and compact, and the solid gilding upon the edges is worthy of commendation; his dentelle borders are fine, but unfortunately he was not careful of the trenchant steel. Padeloup's tooling or ornaments consist chiefly of small dots, and the forms he invented are elegant. When met with in good state, they look like gold lace upon the sides and backs of the books.

The bindings of books which belonged to De Thou are highly prized. He possessed a magnificent library, mostly bound in smooth deep-toned red, yellow, and green morocco. De Thou died in 1617. The Chevalier D'Eon used to bind books in a sort of Etruscan calf, the ornaments on which were copied from the Etruscan vases. The use of the black and red dyes have very frequently corroded the leather.

We must now resume our account of binding in England.

During the early part of the last century the general bindings were, with the exception of what was called Cambridge binding, (from being executed at that place,) of a depreciated character, many of them very clumsy, and devoid of taste in their ornament. Toward the middle some degree of atten-

tion had begun to be paid to the improvement of
bindings, the general kinds being, up to the end of
the eighteenth century, nearly all executed to one
pattern,—viz.: the sides marbled, the backs coloured
brown, with morocco lettering-pieces, and gilt.

The artists of the earlier part of the period of
which we have been treating must have been numerous; but few are known. Two German binders,
of the name of Baumgarten and Benedict, were of
considerable note and in extensive employment in
London during the early part of this century. The
bindings of Oxford were also very good at this
period. Who the distinguished parties at Oxford
were has not been recorded; but a person of the
name of Dawson, then living at Cambridge, has the
reputation of being a clever artist, and may be pronounced as the binder of many of the substantial
volumes still possessing the distinctive binding we
have before referred to. Baumgarten and Benedict
would, doubtless, be employed in every style of
binding of their day, but the chief characteristics of
their efforts are good substantial volumes in russia,
with marbled edges.

To these succeeded Mr. John Mackinlay and two
other Binders, named Kalthœber and Staggemier;
but to Mackinlay may, perhaps, be attributed the

first impulse given to the improvements which have
been introduced into bindings. He was one of the
largest and most creditable binders in London of
the period of which we are treating. Several specimens of his, in public and private libraries, remain
to justify the character given of him; and of the
numerous artists that his office produced, many have
since given evidence, by their work, that the lessons
they received were of a high character. The specimens alluded to exhibit a degree of care, ingenuity,
and skill, highly creditable to them as binders.
Though well executed, they did not pay the time and
attention devoted, in later times, to the finishing or
gilding of their work, and it was not till Roger
Payne exhibited the handiwork of the craft, that
any decided impulse was given to the progress of
the art, which has gone on, under able successors,
from one improvement to another till there exists
much doubt whether or no we have not now, so far
as mechanical execution depends, arrived at perfection. About the year 1770 Roger Payne went to
London, and, as his history is an epoch in the history
of the art, we will devote some space to it.

The personal history of Roger Payne is one
among the many of the ability of a man being rendered nearly useless by the dissoluteness of his

habits. He stands an example to the young, of
mere talent, unattended with perseverance and
industry, never leading to distinction,—of great
ability, clouded by intemperance and consequent
indiscretion, causing the world only to regret how
much may have been lost that might have been
developed had the individual's course been different
and his excellences directed so as to have produced
the best results.

Roger Payne was a native of Windsor Forest, and
first became initiated in the rudiments of the art he
afterward became so distinguished a professor of,
under the auspices of Mr. Pote, bookseller to Eton
College. From this place he went to London, where
he was first employed by Mr. Thomas Osborne, the
bookseller, of Holborn, London. Disagreeing on
some matters, he subsequently obtained employment
from Mr. Thomas Payne, of the King's Mews, St.
Martin's, who ever after proved a friend to him.
Mr. Payne established him in business near Leices-
ter Square, about the year 1769–70, and the
encouragement he received from his patron, and
many wealthy possessors of libraries, was such that
the happiest results and a long career of prosperity
might have been anticipated. His talents as an
artist, particularly in the finishing department, were

of the first order, and such as, up to his time, had not been developed by any other of his countrymen.

He adopted a style peculiarly his own, uniting a classical taste in the formation of his designs, and much judgment in the selection of such ornament as was applicable to the nature of the work it was to embellish. Many of these he made himself of iron, and some are yet preserved as curiosities and specimens of the skill of the man. To this occupation he may have been at times driven from lack of money to procure them from the tool-cutters; but it cannot be set down as being generally so, for, in the formation of the designs in which he so much excelled, it is but reasonable to suppose, arguing upon the practice of some others in later times, he found it readier and more expedient to manufacture certain lines, curves, &c. on the occasion. Be this as it may, he succeeded in executing binding in so superior a manner as to have no rival and to command the admiration of the most fastidious book-lover of his time. He had full employment from the noble and wealthy, and the estimation his bindings are still held in is a sufficient proof of the satisfaction he gave his employers. His best work is in Earl Spencer's library.

His reputation as an artist of the greatest merit was obscured, and eventually nearly lost, by his intemperate habits.   He loved drink better than meat.   Of this propensity an anecdote is related of a memorandum of money spent, and kept by himself, which runs thus:—

> For bacon . . . . 1 halfpenny.
> For liquor . . . . 1 shilling.

No wonder then, with habits like these, that the efforts of his patron, in fixing him, were rendered of no avail.   Instead of rising to that station his great talent would have led to, he fell by his dissolute conduct to the lowest depths of misery and wretchedness.   In his wretched working-room was executed the most splendid specimens of binding; and here on the same shelf were mixed together old shoes and precious leaves—bread and cheese, with the most valuable and costly of MSS. or early-printed books.

That he was characteristic or eccentric may be judged by what has been related of him.   He appears to have also been a poet on the subject of his unfortunate propensity, as the following extract from a copy of verses sent with a bill to Mr. Evans, for binding " Barry on the Wines of the Ancients," proves.

"Homer the bard, who sung in highest strains
   The festive gift, a goblet for his pains ;
   Falernian gave Horace, Virgil fire,
   And Barley Wine my British Muse inspire.
   Barley Wine first from Egypt's learned shore ;
   And this the gift to me of Calvert's *store*."

The following bill is, like himself, a curiosity : —

" Vanerii Praedium Rusticum. Parisiis. MDCCLXXIV.
   Bound in the very best manner in the finest Green Morocco,
   The back lined with Red Morrocco.
" Fine Drawing paper and very neat Morrocco
   Joints inside.   Their was a few leaves stained   } 0 : 0 : 6
   at the foredge, which is washed and cleaned...

" The subject of the Book being Rusticum, I
have ventured to putt The Vine Wreath on it.
I hope I have not bound it in too rich a manner
for the Book.   It takes up a great deal of time
to do these Vine Wreaths.   I guess within Time
I am certain of measuring and working the
different and various small tools required to fill
up the Vine Wreath that it takes very near 3
days' work in finishing the two sides only of the
Book—but I wished to do my best for the Work—
and at the same time I cannot expect to charge a
full and proper price for the Work, and hope that
the price will not only be found reasonable but
cheap . . . . 0 : 18 : 0"

3

Roger commenced business in partnership with his brother Thomas Payne, and subsequently was in like manner connected with one Richard Weir, but did not long agree with either, so that separation speedily took place. He afterward worked under the roof of Mr. Mackinlay, but his later efforts showed that he had lost much of that ability he had been so largely endowed with. Pressed down with poverty and disease, he breathed his last in Duke's Court, St. Martin's Lane, on the 20th of November, 1797. His remains were interred in the burying-ground of St. Martin's-in-the-Fields, at the expense of Mr. Thomas Payne, who, as before stated, had been his early friend, and who, for the last eight years of his life, had rendered him a regular pecuniary assistance both for the support of his body and the performance of his work.

Of the excellencies and defects of his bindings, Dr. Dibdin, in his "Bibliographer's Decameron," has thus recorded his opinion :—

"The great merit of Roger Payne lay in his taste — in his choice of ornaments, and especially in the working of them. It is impossible to excel him in these two particulars. His favourite colour was that of *olive*, which he called *Venetian*. In his lining, joints, and inside ornaments, our hero

generally, and sometimes melancholily, failed. He
was fond of what he called purple paper, the colour
of which was as violent as its texture was coarse.
It was liable also to change and become spotty, and
as a harmonizing colour with olive it was odiously
discordant. The joints of his books were generally
disjointed, uneven, carelessly tooled, and having
a very unfinished appearance. His backs are
boasted of for their firmness. His work excel-
lently forwarded—every sheet fairly and *bona fide*
stitched into the back, which was afterward usually
coated in russia; but his minor volumes did not
open well in consequence. He was too fond of thin
boards, which, in folios, produces an uncomfortable
effect, from fear of their being inadequate to sustain
the weight of the envelop."

Though Roger Payne's career had not been successful, so far as he was personally concerned, it
had the effect of benefiting the whole race of English bookbinders. A new stimulus had been given
to the trade, and a new and chastened style introduced among the more talented artists of the metro-
polis. The unmeaning ornaments we have before
alluded to were discarded, and a series of classical,
geometrical, and highly-finished designs adopted.
The contemporaries of Roger—Kalthœber, Stag-

gemier, Walther, Hering, Falkner, &c.—exerted
themselves with a generous rivalry to execute the
most approved bindings.

Mr. Mackenzie deserves to be mentioned with
respect among modern binders. Charles Lewis, so
highly eulogized by Mr. Dibdin, attained great
celebrity, and his bindings are much prized. His
style of ornament was very neat, the panels of the
backs generally double-mitred, and the sides finished
in a corresponding manner. Mr. Clarke deserves
especial commendation; for tree-marbled calf he
stands unrivalled, although Mr. Riviere has executed
some beautiful specimens. Mr. Bedford also enjoys
considerable reputation; but it is to Mr. Hayday
that the leading position among the London artists
is now generally assigned. His quaint old-fashioned
morocco bindings are inimitable. Lady Willoughby's
Diary has been extensively copied, but not equalled.
His Bibles and Prayer Books are well forwarded;
the edges are solidly gilt with gold of a very deep
colour, while the finishing is rich and massive without
being gaudy. A book in the library of J. W. King
Eyton, Esq., bound by Hayday, is thus described:—

"The work is a large paper copy of the late Mr.
Blakeway's 'Sheriffs of Shropshire,' in imperial
folio, with the armorial bearings beautifully coloured.

The binding is of blood-coloured morocco, extending an inch and a half all round the inside of the
cover, on which is placed a bold but open border
tooled in gold, forming a fine relief to the rest of
the inside, which is in purple, elegantly worked all
over in hexagons running into each other in the
Venetian style. In each compartment is placed the
lion rampant and fleur-de-lis alternately. The fly-
leaves are of vellum, ornamented with two narrow
gold lines, and the edges are tooled. The back
consists of hexagons, inlaid with purple, containing
the lion and fleur-de-lis aforesaid, but somewhat
smaller than those in the interior. The design on
the outside is a triumphal arch, occupying the entire
side, highly enriched, with its cornices, mouldings,
&c. executed in suitable small ornamental work;
from its columns, (which are wreathed with laurel,)
and other parts of the structure, are suspended the
shields of the Sheriffs, seventy in number, the
quarterings of which, with their frets, bends, &c.,
are curiously inlaid in different colours of morocco,
and, with the ornamental parts of the bearings,
have been blazoned with heraldic accuracy on both
sides of the volume. When we state that more than
57,000 impressions of tools have been required to
produce this wonderful exemplar of ingenuity and

3*

skill, some idea may be formed of the time and labour necessary for its execution."

This volume was finished by Thomas Hussey, who is now employed in Philadelphia, and who has in his possession the patterns executed upon the sides and back.

The French degenerated in binding from the time of Louis XIV. until they became far inferior to the English. This continued to the beginning of the present century; the books bound for the Emperor Napoleon, upon which no expense appears to have been spared, are clumsy, disjointed, and the tools coarse and unevenly worked. They were generally bound in red morocco, with morocco joints, lined with purple silk, upon which the imperial bee was stamped repeatedly. Thouvenin enjoys the honour of rescuing the art from its long-continued degradation in France, and of founding a school whose disciples are now acknowledged to rank with the great masters of the art. His tools and patterns were designed and cut by artists in his employ; his establishment was on a large scale; but at his death he left nothing behind him but his reputation as an artist, to stimulate others to attain excellence in workmanship and a cultivated taste in ornament and design. Among the most celebrated binders of

the present day in France are, Trautz et Bauzonnet,
Niédré, Duru, Capé and Lortic. The books of
these artists are distinguished for solidity, squareness, freedom of the joints, firmness of the heads
and back, and extreme nicety of finish. The fore-
edges are gilt with the round in them, giving them
a solid rich appearance, as yet unequalled. The material employed is of the choicest kind,—soft, rich
Levant morocco being the favourite covering for
choice books. This leather, in the hands of an
ordinary workman, would make a clumsy covering
upon account of its great thickness; for it cannot
be shaved down by a skin-dresser without destroy-
ing the natural grain of the leather, and, with it, its
velvet-like richness and beauty; and yet, under the
manipulations of these French artists, it becomes one
of the most plastic of materials; rare volumes of the
smallest dimensions, containing but one or two
sheets, are not only covered on the exterior, but the
interior of the boards, and even the joints are of
Levant morocco. There are many specimens of
binding executed in France for gentlemen of taste
and lovers of the art in this country; and, in speaking of the productions of French artists, it is to
these that we refer. As a binder, Lortic appears
to be the least known; but he will probably ·become

more so. Capé is rapidly growing into favour. Duru
is celebrated for the excellence of his forwarding.
In this respect he cannot be surpassed. The full
morocco specimens that we have seen have generally
been bound *à la Janseniste*, and were truly exemplars.
In exterior gilding he is not so happy as some of his
brethren. Niédré possesses fine taste; his styles
of finishing are varied and graceful in design, and
the execution admirable. The reputation of Trautz
et Bauzonnet has been established principally by
the senior partner, Bauzonnet, Trautz being his son-
in-law, and whose name has recently been placed at
the head of the firm, perhaps to anticipate others in
claiming to be the inheritors of the skill, and pupils
of his father-in-law's school. Bauzonnet's bindings
combine excellence in every department. They are
specimens of the art in its highest state, being solid,
firm, and square in every portion of the forwarding
department. The covering, joints, and inside linings
are matchless. The finishing may safely be pronounced perfection, so far as any thing produced
by human agency can be. In style of finishing he
generally confines himself to modifications of the
Grolier, or to a broad border, composed of fine
tools; and in the tooling the execution is faultless.
Those who are accustomed to English bindings are

apt to find fault with the firmness of his backs, as they do not throw out like English loose backs; but this subject of loose backs is but little understood; for, when it is known that what is generally esteemed an excellence is often but an indication of weakness,—that, in order to make the book throw out and lie open flat, the substance by which the sheets are secured together is a single strip of paper,—and that, where the band upon which the book is sewn can be plainly seen upon the opening of the volume, there is a strain upon it, the result of which must be its breakage, if in constant use, (a catastrophe that will never happen to one of Bauzonnet's books,)—the firm back will be preferred. In tracing the progress of the Art, and upon comparing the merits of artists of ancient and modern times, it is to the moderns that we assign the palm of superiority, especially for perfection of detail in the ornamentation.

MANUAL

OF THE

ART OF BOOKBINDING.

PART I.

SHEET WORK.

As the gathering of the sheets of a book, after they have been printed and dried off, is nearly always performed at the printer's, it will not be necessary to enter into any details on that subject, but to consider, as the commencement of binding, the operation of

FOLDING,

which is of great importance, the beauty of a book depending on its being properly and correctly folded, so that, when it is cut, the margin of the different pages may be uniform throughout, and present no transpositions, to the inconvenience of the reader and deterioration of the work.

The various sizes of books are denominated

according to the number of leaves in which the
sheet is folded; as folio, quarto, octavo, 12mo,
16mo, 18mo, 24mo, 32mo, &c. Each form presents a certain number of pages, so disposed that,
when the sheet is properly folded, they will follow
the numeric order. In commencing the folding
of any work, particular attention should be paid,
in opening out the quires or sets, to observe that
the *signatures* follow each other alphabetically,
and, if consisting of two or more volumes, that the
whole of the sheets belong to the right one.

Although each form is folded in a different manner, it will not be requisite to detail the whole, as a
description of the octavo and twelvemo will amply
furnish an idea of the proper way of folding the
larger and smaller sizes.

Octavo.—The sheets being placed on the table
with the signature, which will be seen at the bottom
of the first page, turned towards the table at the
corner nearest to the left hand of the workman,
will present pages 2, 15, 14, 3, below, and above,
with their heads reversed, pages 7, 10, 11, 6,
(reading from left to right.) The sheet is then
taken with the left hand, by the angle to the right,
and creased with the *folder* in the right hand, in
the direction of the *points* made in the printing,

taking care, by shading to the light, that the figures
of the pages fall exactly one on the other, which
will be 3 upon 2, and 6 upon 7, and thereby presenting uppermost pages 4 and 13, and above 5 and
12. The top part of the sheet is then brought
down, with the left hand, upon the lower, pages 5
and 12 falling upon 4 and 13, directed properly,
and again folded. The sheet then presents pages
8 and 9, which are then folded evenly, 9 upon 8,
forming the third fold and finishing the sheet.

Twelvemo.—The signature to this size, when
placed before the workman, should be at the top,
on his left hand, and towards the table, the sheet
presenting pages 2, 7, 11; 23, 18, 14; 22, 19, 15;
3, 6, 10. On the right, pages 11, 14, 15, 10, are
separated from the others by a larger space, in the
middle of which are the points, indicating the
proper place where the pages should be cut off.
The *folder* detaches this part, and, placing page 11
upon 10, makes a fold, and 13 upon 12, which will
be uppermost, finishes the folding of what is called
the *inset*, and which bears the signature of the
sheet it has been separated from, with the addition
of a figure or asterisk, as A 5 or A*. The remaining eight pages are folded in the same way as the
octavo, and when done the inset is placed in the

4

middle of it, taking care that the head-lines arrange properly.

Books are sometimes printed in what is called half sheets, but they are folded the same, after cutting them up; the octavo in the direction of the points, the twelvemo in *oblong* direction of the paper, and laying them apart from each other. There are also oblong octavos, which are folded in the middle in a line with the points, the second fold in the same direction between the heads of the pages, and the third on the length of the paper.

In the first fold of the octavo sheet is shown the manner of folding the folio, and in the second the quarto; the twelvemo also presents us with the eighteens, after the sheet is cut into three divisions. Little or no difficulty will be experienced in folding any other size that may occur, attention to the disposition of the pages and signatures being only required.

It will often be found necessary to refold a book which, previous to being bound, may have been done up in boards, sewed, or otherwise. This should in all cases be carefully attended to, after the book has been taken to pieces, the back divested of the glue and thread, and the corners or other parts which may have been doubled turned up.

This is usually done by examining if the margin at the head and fore-edge is equal throughout, bringing those to their proper place that are too short, and cutting those that are longer than the general margin. By these means a uniformity will be presented after the edges of the book are cut, which could never be attained if not attended to while the book is in this state.

The sheets of the book, being all folded, are then laid out along the edge of the gathering table, in the regular order of the signatures; the gatherer then commences at the last sheet or signature, takes one sheet from the parcel, one from the next, and so on until the first sheet or title is placed upon the top of the rest. The sheets are then held loosely in the hand, and allowed to fall lightly upon their backs and heads upon a smooth board, until they arrange themselves in an even, uniform manner. They are then

COLLATED,

to see that the whole of the sheets belong to the same work and volume, as also that none are wanting. This is done by taking the book in the right hand by the upper corner of the fore-edge, and with the left opening the sheets on the back and

letting them fall successively one after the other.
The signatures will be thus seen in alphabetical or
arithmetical order, as A, B, C, &c., or 1, 2, 3, 4,
&c., to the last, which should always be examined
to ascertain that it is the completion of the book.
By these means any sheet incorrectly folded is also
detected. Books in folio and quarto are generally
collated with a needle or pricker, by raising the
sheets singly from the table; but this practice
should be resorted to as little as possible, as the
work is liable to be damaged. If any sheet is
wanting, or belongs to another volume, or is a duplicate, the further progress of the work must be suspended till the imperfection is procured or ex-
changed. Those that have been wrong folded
must be corrected, and any *cancels* occurring in the
work cut out and replaced by the reprints, which
will generally be found in the last sheet of the
book. It is usual also with some binders to place
any plates belonging to the volume, at this period;
but as the liability of damage to them is great in
the process of *beating*, or rolling, it will be much
better to perform that operation after the book is
brought from the stone, for which directions will be
given. The book, being found correct, will be
ready for the beating-stone, which, although it has

been almost entirely superseded by the introduction
of machinery, will always be invaluable to a binder
of limited means ; and the amateur will find it to
be an essential process to secure the first great
requisite of good binding,—solidity

BEATING, PRESSING, ETC.

The first operation is commenced by shaking the
volume upon the stone by the back and head, so as
to make the whole even and facilitate the division
of it into as many equal parts, which are called
sections or *beatings*, as may be judged necessary according to the thickness and other circumstances.
A section is then taken and well beaten over, drawing it with the hand towards the body so as to bring
the various parts successively under the hammer,
and carefully avoiding striking more blows in one
part than the other, except giving the edges a slight
extra tap round. The section is then turned, and
the like proceeding gone through; as also on each
side after it has been separated and the bottom part
placed on the top, the middle of the section being
thereby brought under the action of the hammer.
This being done, the sheets are replaced in their
proper order, and two or three taps of the hammer
given to make them lie even. In beating those

4*

books with which, from their value, greater care is
required, it is usual to place a guard or waste leaf
of paper on each side of the section, to avoid any
stains or marks which the stone or hammer might be
liable to make.

It requires more skill than actual strength in
beating, the weight of the hammer being nearly
sufficient for many works. Attention must be paid
to the hammer descending parallel to the surface of
the stone, to avoid marking or cutting the sheets
with the edge.

Before beating a book, care should be taken to
observe if it has been recently printed, for if so it
would *set off* by being beaten too much. This will
be easily ascertained by referring to the date at the
foot of the title, or by smelling the ink it has been
printed with, which, being composed partly of oil,
will not have got perfectly dry. This will particularly be the case with machine-printed works. As,
however, it is frequently necessary to bind a volume
immediately after being printed, it will be requisite

to take every precaution against its setting off, which would destroy the beauty of the work. It is the practice of some to put the book into an oven after the bread has been taken out, or into a stove heated sufficiently to dry the ink and make it search into the paper; but, as these means are not without danger of getting the paper blackened or soiled, it is a better plan to interleave the sheets with white paper, which will receive all the ink set off. Should the sheets have been hotpressed, which is readily distinguished, this precaution will not be necessary.

When employed at the beating-stone, the workman should keep his legs close together, to avoid *hernia*, to which he is much exposed if, with the intention of being more at ease, he contracts the habit of placing them apart.

A rolling-machine has been invented as a substitute for the beating which books require previous to being bound. The book is divided into parts, according to the thickness of the book; each part is then placed between tins, or pieces of sole-leather; the rollers are then put in motion, and the part passed through. This is repeated until the requisite degree of solidity is obtained. The great objections to the rolling-machine are the liabilities to cause a set-off, or transfer of the printing-ink, upon the opposite

page, by the friction which is produced by passing
between the rollers, and the bow-like appearance
which they give the book, and which is to the
forwarder a serious cause of annoyance, and sometimes all his skill and care are insufficient to remedy
the evil caused by the rollers.

A powerful embossing press, technically called a
smasher, has lately been employed with great advantage. A book is placed between tins, the platen
is adjusted to a proper height, and the large fly-
wheels set in motion. The platen descends in a
perpendicular manner; then, upon its ascending, by
means of a small handle the distance between the
platens is decreased; the wheels still continuing in
motion, the book, upon the descent of the platen, is
compressed more forcibly than at first. The operation is repeated until the book has experienced
the whole power of the press. It has been calculated that by this process a single volume will, if
necessary, undergo a pressure equal to a weight of
from fifty to eighty tons.

This process has an advantage over every other
hitherto employed in which machinery has been engaged; and it is, in some respects, preferable to
beating, as the book is of the same thickness in
every part, while in beating there is a great liability

to beat the edges thinner than the centre ; and the air appears to be as completely forced out as if the beating-hammer had been used; and there seems to be no disposition in the book to swell up again after undergoing this crushing process.

In some binderies a hydraulic press is relied upon for compressing the sheets, without their undergoing the beating or rolling process. For publishers' work it has been found to answer the purpose for which it is employed, as the press can be filled up by placing the books in layers of from one to four or eight, according to their size, between iron plates; and the immense power of the press is thus evenly distributed through a large quantity of sheets at the same time.

The power of compression is derived from the pump to the left of the press, which is supplied with water from a cistern sunk under it. The water thus sent, by means of the tube seen passing from it to the centre of the foot of the press, causes the cylinder to which the bed is fixed to rise and compress the books or paper tightly between the bed and head of the press. When it is forced as high as can be by means of the pump-handle seen, a larger bar is attached and worked by two men. The extraordinary power

HYDRAULIC PRESS, FROM THE MANUFACTORY OF
ISAAC ADAMS & CO., BOSTON.

of this press is so great as to cause, particularly in common work, a saving of more than three-fourths of the time required in bringing books to a proper solidity by the common press. When it is wished to withdraw the books, the small cock at the end of the tube at the foot of the press is turned, the water flows into the cistern below, and the bed with the books glides gently down in front of the workman. Two presses are frequently worked by the same pump, one being on each side.

The hydraulic press is manufactured by nearly all the press-makers, differing only in the general design, the application of power being the same.

After beating, should there be any plates to the work, they, as before stated, must now be placed among the text. Great care must be taken to make the justification of the plates uniform with the text, by cutting off any superfluity at the head or back, and by placing them exactly facing the pages to which they refer, pasting the edge next to the back. Any that may be short at the head must be brought down, to preserve a uniformity. It is advisable to place a leaf of *tissue-paper* before each plate, particularly when newly printed, as the ink of copper-plates is longer in drying than that of letter-press. When a work contains a great number of plates, which are directed to be placed at the end, they are sewn on the bands by over-casting, which operation will shortly be treated of in full.

The book, being now ready for pressing, is taken in sections, according to the work and the judgment of the workman, and placed between pressing-boards the size of the volume, one on the other, and conveyed to the *standing-press*, which is pulled down as tight as possible by the *press-pin*, or fly-wheel, according to the nature of the standing-press; although it must be premised that when a book has been through the smasher, no further pressing will be required until it reaches the hands of the forwarder.

After the book has been sufficiently pressed, it will be necessary again to *collate* it, to correct any disarrangement that may have taken place during the beating and pressing. It is then ready for being sawn out.

SAWING THE BACKS.

This operation is performed in order to save the expense of sewing upon raised bands, and also to prevent the bands on which a book is sewn appear-ing on the back. After beating the book up well on the back and head, it is placed between two *cutting-boards*, the back projecting a little over the thick edge, and tightly screwing in the *laying* or *cutting-press*, the whole being elevated sufficiently to prevent the saw damaging the checks of the press. Then with a *tenant-saw* the proper number of grooves are made, in depth and width according to the diameter of the band intended to be used, which will depend on the size of the book. A slight cut must also be given above the first and under the last band, for lodging the *chain* or *kettle-stitch*. It is very necessary that the saw should be held parallel with the press, without which precaution, the grooves being deeper on one side than the other, the work will present, when opened, a defect to the eye.

The *end-papers*, which should consist of four leaves of blank paper, folded according to the size of the book, are now prepared, and one placed at the beginning and end of each volume.

SEWING.

According to the number of *bands* wanted, must be attached to the loops on the cross-bar of the *sewing-press* as many pieces of cord, of proper length and thickness, and fastened with the aid of the *keys* in the groove of the press as nearly equal

5

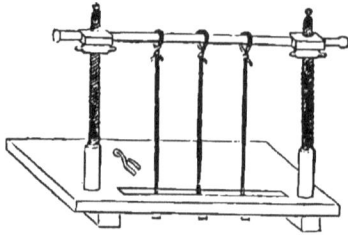

in tightness as possible. When this is done, the
back of the first sheet in the book is placed against
the cords, which must be moved upwards or the
contrary to the marks of the saw, when the small
screws at each end under the cross-bar must be
moved upwards till the strings are equally tight.
All this being disposed, the book is commenced sewing by placing the end-paper, which has no marks
of the saw, on the sheet before laid down, and sewing it throughout, leaving a small end of thread to
form the knot, after sewing the first sheet, which is
then taken from under and sewn the whole length.

There are various ways of sewing, according to
the size and thickness of the sheets of a book. A
volume consisting of thick sheets, or a sheet containing a plate or map, should be sewn singly the
whole length, in order to make the work more
secure and solid. Great care should also be taken
not to draw the thread too tight at the head or foot

of the book. The thread, in order to keep the book of the same thickness at the ends and centre, should be drawn parallel with the bench, and not downwards, as is too frequently the case. Upon the proper swelling of the back mainly depends the regularity of the round and firmness of the back in the after-stages of the binding.

When a book is sewed *two sheets on*, three bands are generally used. Taking the sheet and fixing it on the bands, the needle is inserted in the mark made for the kettle-stitch and brought out by the first band; another sheet is then placed, and the needle introduced on the other side of the band, thus bringing the thread round it, sewn in like manner to the middle band, and continued to the third, when, taking again the first sheet, it is sewn from the third band to the other kettle-stitch, where it is fastened, and another course of two sheets commenced, and so continued to the last sheet but one, which is sewn the whole length, as directed for the first sheet, as also the end-paper. Three bands are preferable to two, the book being more firm from being fastened in the middle, which is the only difference in sewing on two and three bands.

Half-sheets, to obviate the swelling of the back too much, are usually sewn on four bands, which

admit of three on a course: the first sheet is sewn
as in three bands, from the kettle-stitch to the first
band, the next to the second, and the third takes
the middle space ; then the second sheet again from
the third to the fourth band, and the first from
thence to the other kettle-stitch. The third sheet
having only one stitch, it is necessary that, in sawing, the distance from the second to the third band
should be left considerably longer than between the
others.   Quartos are generally sewn on five bands
to make the work firmer, but if in half-sheets, as in
the folio size, six or more are used, sewing as many
sheets on as bands, giving each sheet but one tack
or sewing, and piercing the needle through the
whole of the course at each end or kettle-stitch
before fastening the thread. This, which gives
sufficient firmness, is necessary to prevent the swelling of the back which a less number of sheets in a
course would make and spoil the appearance of the
binding.

When the book is composed of single leaves,
plates, or maps, or, as in the case of music, where,
from the decayed state of the back, it is necessary
to cut off a portion with the plough in the manner
pointed out for cutting edges, the whole must be
attached to the bands by what is called whipping or

overcasting. This is by taking a section, according to the thickness of the paper, and forcing the needle through the whole at the kettle-stitch, and on each side of all the bands, at a distance sufficient to secure the stitches from tearing, bringing the thread round each band, as before directed, and fastening it at the end before proceeding with another course. To keep the whole of the sheets properly even, the back is sometimes glued immediately after cutting, and when dry divided into sections. Atlases and books of prints, when folded in the middle, will require a guard, or slip of paper, to be pasted to them, so as to allow them to open flat, which they could not do if attached to the back, and which would destroy the engraving. These guards must be of strong paper about an inch in breadth and folded to the right size. They are sewn by overcasting, as above directed.

A better method for books of plates, or single leaves, is, after cutting the back evenly with the plough, to lay it between boards and glue the back evenly over with thin glue. After it has become dry and hard, separate it into thin sections; then let it be sawn out in the usual manner; it should then be taken and whipped, or overcast in separate sections with fine thread, care being taken in

5*

whipping the sections that it be evenly and neatly
done.   After the sections are all whipped, they
should be sewn or affixed to the bands in the same
manner as folded sheets.

The old mode of sewing on raised bands combines many advantages.   This style is still adopted
with many works, particularly with those having
a small margin ; in fact, it is, both for elasticity
and durability, far superior to any mode that
is practised; it is, however, a very slow process, and necessarily an expensive one ; and many
binders who pretend to bind in this manner, to
obviate this, have their books sewed in the ordinary way, and then, by sticking false bands upon
the back, give them the appearance of having been
sewn on raised bands.   If it is intended to sew
a book purely flexible, it should be knocked up even
and square, placed between two pieces of pasteboard, and placed in a laying-press; then draw a
line across the back, near the head, where it will be
cut by the forwarder in cutting the edges.   Next
take a pair of compasses and divide the back
lengthwise into six even portions, except the bottom
or tail, which should be longer than the rest, in
order to preserve a proper symmetry of appearance ; then draw lines square across the back with

a black lead-pencil from the compass-points of the five inner divisions, for the places upon which the bands are to be sewed; then make a slight scratch with a saw about one-quarter of an inch inside of where the book will be cut, for the kettle-stitch at the head and likewise at the tail. Upon taking the book out of the laying-press, take the pasteboards and saw them at the points marked by the lead-pencil of a depth sufficient to allow the cords upon which the book is to be sewn to enter. The boards will then serve as a guide to set the bands of the sewing-press at the commencement of the operation, and afterwards, during the progress of the work, will be found useful to regulate any deviations that may be inadvertently taking place. After the sewing-press is properly regulated and the end-paper sewn as previously described, the sheets should then be taken, one at a time, in their regular order, and sewn all along, from one end of the sheet to the other, or, more properly, from one kettle-stitch to the other, taking especial pains to observe that in sewing each sheet, after the first kettle-stitch has been caught, the needle must be passed to the farthest side of the nearest band, then passed to the other side of the band, and so on for each successive band. By this means the

thread will have passed completely round each
band, upon which the sheet will revolve as upon
a hinge, without the slightest strain upon either the
band or the thread. The inner margin is thus
preserved its full size, and the freedom of the
volume much increased.

If you desire to revel in the full enjoyment of a
flexible back, have it sewn with silk upon silken
bands or cords, and you will have a combination of
elasticity and strength that cannot be surpassed.

For large volumes of engravings, the best mode
of binding, so as to secure strength and also to
allow the plates to lie flat when the volume is open,
is to mount the plates with linen upon guards. To
do this properly, select paper of the same thickness
as the plates, cut it in strips an inch or an inch and
a half wide, paste the back edge of the plate about
a quarter of an inch in depth, from top to bottom;
then lay a strip of thin linen or paper-muslin along
the pasted edge of the plate, and rub it so that it
will adhere. The strips of linen must be sufficiently
wide to project beyond the plate as far as the width
of the paper guards. One of the latter is then to
be evenly pasted over and laid upon the projecting
strip of linen, carefully smoothed, and laid between
pasteboards to dry after they are thus mounted.

The plates are then whipped along the back edge of the guard, and sewed in the usual manner.

It was proposed by *M. Lesne*, bookbinder of *Paris*, in a Memoir presented by him to the "*Societé d'Encouragement*," January 18, 1818, that in order to give to books the three essential qualities of binding, elasticity, solidity, and elegance, they should be sewn similar to the Dutch method, which is on slips of parchment, instead of packthread; but to remedy the inconvenience arising from one slip being insufficient to make the back of a proper solidity, as well as being liable to break, and, if doubled or trebled, presenting a bad effect on the back when covered, he suggested the adoption of silk for the bands, which in a much less diameter is far stronger than packthread double the thickness. It is also preferable for sheets that require sewing the whole length to use silk, this being much stronger than thread, and insuring a greater solidity to the work. It will be observed that the cuts of the saw, apparent in other bindings, are not seen in opening the volume. When the volume is entirely sewn, the screws are loosened, the cords detached from the keys, and about two inches of the cord left on each side of the book to attach the boards that are to form the sides.

INDIA-RUBBER BACKS.

In those instances where the leaves of a book are held together by caoutchouc cement instead of by sewing, the sheets are cut up into separate leaves, and every leaf made true and square at the edges. The back edge is then brought to a rounded form, by allowing the sheets to arrange themselves in a grooved recess or mould; and in that state the leaves are all moistened at the back edges with a cement of liquid caoutchouc or India-rubber. The quantity so applied is very small. In a few hours, it is sufficiently dry to take another coat of a somewhat stronger caoutchouc solution. In forty-eight hours, four applications of the caoutchouc may be made and dried. The back and the adjoining part of the sides are next covered with the usual band or fillet of cloth glued on with caoutchouc; after which the book is ready to have the boards attached, and to be covered with leather or parchment, as may be desired.

PART II.

FORWARDING.

This branch of the art may be divided into several parts. We will give precedence to that branch or class of forwarding that requires the utmost precision and opens to the ambitious forwarder a field of exertion worthy of his best efforts. Let the workman who strives to excel in his art remember that his work goes through the hands of critics and judges; that it possibly may be compared with the productions of the most celebrated artists. Let him, then, look well to his laurels if engaged upon first-class job or

CUSTOMER WORK.

The book being taken from the sewing-press, the end-papers and the first sheet are then turned back. A strip of paper is placed about one-eighth of an inch from the back, so as to prevent the paste from spreading unevenly, and paste is then applied with the finger along the edge of the sheet. The sheet is turned over, and the same process repeated to the first and second leaves of the end-papers, if the

book is to be lined with buff or brown paper.
After the papers have been cut to the proper size
and evenly folded, they are pasted along the folded
edge in the same manner as the end-papers were.
The first leaf of the end-paper is then turned over,
and the lining-paper laid full up to the back-edge
of the book.   If this be done carelessly, or not entirely straight and square from end to end, the
future appearance of the book will be considerably
marred.   As much of the beauty of the joint
depends upon the manner in which the lining has
been performed, if it is intended to line with marbled
paper, after turning over the end-leaf, place the
lining as near as possible to the back-edge, so as to
expose to the action of the brush almost the entire
leaf of the end-paper that lies on the book.   Paste
this lightly over; then place the lining upon it, and
rub it even and smooth with the hand.   In either
case it should be left to dry before the end-paper is
folded down to its place, as it is liable to force the
lining-paper from the back.   A better method is to
paste the marble-paper upon the white end-paper
before it is inserted in the book.   The papers may
then be lightly pressed, to make them perfectly
smooth, and hung upon lines to dry.   By this process
there is no fear of the book being wrinkled by the

dampness from the lining-paper. Attention should be paid that such papers only as will blend well with the colour of the leather intended for the cover are used.

If a joint of calf or morocco is required, all that is necessary for the forwarder to do is to tip the back-edge of the lining that goes next to the book very slightly, merely to secure it until it reaches the finisher, and place one or two guards of stout paper along the joint, to be afterwards torn out by the finisher.

These matters being adjusted, the end-paper turned back to its place, and the twine on which the book has been sewn pulled tight, care having been taken to avoid pressing the twine against the end-papers, on account of their liability to tear near the bands, the bands which are intended to be laced in the boards must be opened, or the strands separated with a bodkin and scraped with a dull knife so as to bring them to a point and make them more convenient to pass through the boards which are to form the side covers.

The book is now taken between the hands and well beaten up at the back and head on a smooth board, or on the laying-press, to bring the sheets level and square, as the beauty of the book, in all

6

the subsequent operations, depends much on the care and attention paid in this place. The volume is then laid carefully upon a board, with the back to the edge of the board, a strip of pasteboard is laid on the upper side, the book placed in the laying-press, and the back evenly glued. The glue should be well rubbed in between the sheets, taking care that the sheets are even on the back and the volume equal in thickness throughout the whole length. It is then laid on a board to dry, but must not be placed before the fire, as, by so doing, the glue becomes hard and liable to crack in the process of

ROUNDING.

In commencing this operation, the book is placed upon the laying-press with the fore-edge towards the workman; the left hand should then be placed flat and open upon it, the thumb towards the fore-edge. With the four fingers the volume is slightly bent and the upper portion of the back drawn towards the workman. The right hand is then engaged with a backing-hammer in lightly tapping the sheets with an upward motion from the centre of the back. The volume is then turned upon the other side, and tne operation is repeated until it is evident that the book has acquired a sufficient round. The left hand is held to the back while the round is pressed into the fore-edge with the fingers of the right. The volume is then held up and the back carefully examined to ascertain if the round is perfectly regular, and, if not, it must be again submitted to light blows of the hammer until the back describes a portion of a perfect circle. Care should be taken that the round be not too flat for the thickness of the volume, or, on the other hand, that it does not become what is called a pig-back,—a horrible monstrosity in binding, having a sharp ridge in the centre of the back. If the round be not regular and even from the centre to the edges, as well as from head to tail, and entirely free from twist, no after-skill or care can overcome the evil, but it will ever remain to prove the want of care or the incapacity of the workman. The next process, and equally important, is that of

BACKING,

which is done to form the groove for the reception of the boards. One of the backing-boards is placed upon the volume at an equal distance from the back, the distance depending upon the thickness of the board; then, turning the volume, the other is placed in a

similar manner; the boards are then firmly grasped
by the left hand across the back, and, with the
assistance of the right hand, the whole carefully
put into the laying-press, the edge of the boards
nearest the back of the volume even with the
cheeks of the press, and screwed up with the press-
pin as tight as possible. The backing-hammer is
then taken in the right hand and employed in turning the sheets from the centre over the backing-
boards, to form the necessary groove. For this
purpose the first blows should commence near the
centre of the volume, and should be as light as possible, the blows glancing towards the edge, so as to
merely commence the turning of the sheets, without
causing any indentations or wrinkles on the inside
of the volume. This should be proceeded with
lengthwise of the volume, each series of blows
growing gradually nearer to the edge or backing-
board, and, as they approach, becoming more firm,
until the sheets are turned over the backing-board,
so as to form a regular and solid groove. The process is repeated up the other side, the volume examined to see if the back is regular and equal in its
circle throughout, and any slight irregularities corrected by light taps of the beating-hammer; but
nothing can justify a workman in striking a heavy

blow near the centre of the back, as it must inevi-
tably crush and wrinkle the paper on the inside.
It serves but to prove his ignorance of the principle
upon which the entire operation is based. There is
nothing connected with the forwarding of a book
that requires more attention, patience, and skill,
than the rounding and backing, and there is nothing
that contributes more to the general appearance of
the volume. If well done, it gives a character and
a tone to all the subsequent operations; if done
badly, no care or skill that may be afterwards employed can hide it. It remains an enduring mark
of a careless or inefficient workman. The volume
is now ready for the boards, which have been previously prepared. This is done by cutting the
sheets of milled-boards according to the size of the
book, with the table or patent-shears. One side of
the board is then lined with paper, the shrinkage
of which will cause the board to curl towards it.
If the volume be large, or a thick board be required,
it will be necessary to paste two or more thick-
nesses of board together. Place them in the standing-press, under pressure, until dry; then take
them out and line them on the side of the board
that has been pasted, or, if one board be thinner
than the other, upon the thin board, in the same

manner as the single board. Boards made in this
manner should always be prepared some length of
time before they are used. The boards being in
readiness, the volume is taken and one point of the
compasses placed at the centre of the back, and the
other point extended towards the fore-edge until it
reaches the edge of the smallest bolt. This will
give the proper size to cut the boards, as the groove
or joint will give the projection or square of the
board. If the volume be rare and valuable, let the
workman be merciful in the use of his steel, as the
cropping of ignorant workmen has impaired the
value of many a choice tome. If it be intended
that the leaves are to remain uncut, previous to the
rounding of the volume, take a large butcher's-knife
and carefully trim the extreme ends of the projecting
leaves. After the size has been obtained, the next
operation is

SQUARING THE BOARDS.

This is done by cutting the back-edge of the
boards with a plough in the laying-press; the boards
are then marked with the compasses from the edge
which has been squared towards the front; the front
cutting-board is placed at the compass-holes, and
again put in press, with the front cutting-board or

runner level with the cheek of the press, the back-board being a little higher, so as to allow the plough-knife to cut against it. The rough part is cut off with the plough as hereafter described, with this difference:—that, in cutting pasteboards, the workman cuts towards him. The boards are then taken out of press, and the square applied to the head, and marked with the point of a bodkin; this is cut off in the same manner. The volume is then opened and examined for the purpose of finding a leaf of an average length, which is measured by placing the thumb of the left hand against the edge of the head and applying against it one of the points of the compasses, carrying the other so much over the end of the leaf as will allow for the square of the boards at the tail; and if the volume be large for a portion of the square at the head, the superfluous portion is then cut off with the plough. In taking the size, let the workman recognise as a rule that every book should be cut as large as possible, lest he be suspected of having an eye more to the shaving-tub than to his reputation as a binder. Among the early binders, De Rome is noted for his merciless cropping. But few volumes have preserved the integrity of their margins after having been submitted to the cruel operation of his steel. A volume cut

to the print is said to bleed; therefore be careful to
avoid the slightest approach towards the commission
of such an act of Vandalism. The boards having
been squared for the back, front, head, and tail,
they are placed, with the lined side of the board
next to the book, preparatory to the

LACING IN.

Each board is then marked with a bodkin opposite
to the slips intended to be laced in; a hole in a
vertical position is then made through the board,
and being turned, another in the same way near to
the first. The bands, having been pasted and passed
in above, are returned through the other hole, and,
being pulled tight, the boards will necessarily be
perpendicular to the back, and confined in the
groove. After cutting off the end of the strings
near to the lace-holes, they must be beaten well
and evenly into the board by placing the under
part on an iron (called the *knocking-down iron*)
fixed at the end of the laying-press, and beating
above with the backing-hammer.

If it be desirable that the bands should not be
seen inside, the hole may be made so vertical that,
by placing the bodkin in the same on the other side,
another verging a contrary way to the first may be

made, and the band, being passed in this one continued hole, will not be seen underneath. The
liability, however, of its tearing out is an objection,
and from this cause the common way, with care in
beating down, is preferable.

After the slips have been well beaten down, the
roundness of the back must be examined, and any
twist that is perceptible corrected with the backing-
hammer. A piece of smooth tin, larger than the
volume, must then be inserted between each board
and the book, with one edge of the tin full up to
the joint. The volume is next placed between pressing-boards even with the joint, and put into the
standing-press, which must be screwed tight and
evenly down. Stewart's double-screw iron standing-
press is well adapted for the purpose, and is in very
general use. After the press has been screwed
down, the back of the volume is then damped with
thin paste, and, according to the firmness of the
sewing and book, grated and scraped, and finally
rubbed smooth with paper-shavings, and left to dry
in the press for as long a time as possible. If a
large volume, it is usual to apply a little glue to the
back. When taken out of the press, the boards
must be disengaged from the end-papers, where they

adhere, so that they may move freely up and down
in the cutting.

The manner of preparing the volume for cutting
is very important, as swerving from right angles in
cutting the head and tail will present a disagreeable
appearance. Every precaution must be taken to
insure the volume being cut perfectly square. The
front-board is drawn down from the head just sufficient for the knife to operate upon in the cutting. A
piece of trindle is inserted between the volume and
the back-board for the point of the knife to cut
against. The volume is then placed, with the back
towards the workman, on a cutting-board in the left
hand; the *runner* or smooth-edged board is then
fixed on the other side, with the right hand, even

and square with the edge of the mill-board, and the
whole, held tight with the left hand, put into the

cutting-press, to the level of the right-hand cheek of the same, taking care that the volume hangs perpendicular to the cheeks of the press. Being screwed tight with the pin, the workman then takes the plough with the right hand, by the head of the screw, and, placing it on the groove of the press, proceeds to cut the book, holding the other end of the screw firmly with the left hand, and causing the knife to advance gradually through the book by turning the screw gently as he cuts, which should be all one way,—viz.: as the arms are removed from the body. The plough must be held firm in the groove or guides of the press, to prevent the knife jumping or cutting the edges uneven; and, should the knife be found to run up or down, the defect must be remedied by removing some of the paper or boards placed under the knife where it is fastened to the plough. If there should be none required to bring the knife even with the plough, then a piece must be placed on whichever side of the *bolt* the defect may require. The head being cut, the same operation is repeated for the tail.

Much precaution is necessary in cutting the fore-edge. Mark the book with a bodkin on the projecting part of the end-papers, and on each side, at the head and foot, close to the square side of the boards,

drawing a line from one to the other; then, laying
the boards open, insert a trindle at each end of
the volume, under the back, so as to throw the
round out; then wind a piece of fine cord several
times round from the head to the tail, to prevent
the leaves returning after the back is made flat, to
form the gutter on the fore-edge. This done, beat
the back flat on the press, and place one of the cutting-boards at the end of the book, even with the
line before made : turn it, and place the runner as
much below the line on the title-side as has been
allowed for the square on the fore-edge. Taking
the whole in the left hand, the volume must be examined to remedy any defects, should it not be
regular and equal on both sides, and then put into
the press, the runner as before even with the right
cheek, taking care to keep the other board pro-
jected above the left, equal to the square allowed
in front, so that, when cut through, the fore-edge
may be equally square with the boards on each side.
After the fore-edge is cut, the string is taken off,
the back resumes its circular form, and the edge in
consequence presents a grooved appearance, which
puzzles the uninitiated to ascertain how it is produced. The method above described is called
"cutting in boards," and is superior to any other.

It is of the utmost importance to the young workman that he should pursue and acquire a methodical
system in all his operations. Select the best method,
as a matter of course, and then adhere to it. Do not,
every time you perform one particular process, do it
in a different manner. For instance : in backing or
in turning up your books, it is better to always have
the head towards you; in cutting head and tail, to
have the back nearest you. In laying your work
down, always do it in one way. Let that way be
the one whereby you can most conveniently take it
up again. Much time may be wasted, from inatten-
tion to these particulars, in the unnecessary hand-
ling and confused manner of working. It will be
found that the best and most expeditious workmen
are those who do their work in a systematical manner. In taking leave of this department, our part-
ing admonition to the young workman is, STRIVE TO
EXCEL. Do not be content if your work will merely
pass, and say to yourself, "Oh, that is good enough!"
If it is possible for you to do it better, it is not
good enough. Employ your reasoning faculties as
well as your physical powers, so that you do not
sink into a mere machine. When performing a process, ask yourself the question, "Why is this done?
What is the object of it? Can the process be im-

7

proved?" You will find the hand to be an apt
instrument of the mind and will, and that you will
speedily be recognised as an intelligent workman.
Have, at least, this much ambition.

The next process which the volume must undergo
is the gilding or colouring of

THE EDGES.

Colouring the edges with one colour, equally
sprinkling over, marbling, and gilding, come under
this head; and the style of ornament of this description must depend on the price allowed for the
work, and will vary according to the taste of the
workman and wish of the employer.

OF COLOURING AND SPRINKLING.

The colours most used are brown and red, in
preparing which it is necessary to grind them in
water, very fine, on a slab, with a muller. Each
colour is then placed in a separate vase, and mixed
up with a little paste and water to the proper consistency for use. To procure a better edge, two
drops of oil and about an equal quantity of vinegar
and water may be mixed with the paste.

In colouring the edges equally over, the boards
at the head of the volume must be beat even with
the edges, and the book rested on the edge of the

press or table; then, holding the book firm with the left hand, the colours must be applied with a small sponge or brush, passing it evenly upon the edge, proceeding towards the back one way and the gutter the other, to avoid a mass of colour being lodged in the angle of the fore-edge. This done, the other parts are similarly coloured, the fore-edge being laid open from the boards and a runner held firm above to prevent the colour searching into the book. It will be perceived that a dozen volumes may be done at the same time with scarcely more than the additional trouble of placing one above the other. For further security, and to prevent the colour searching into the books, it is advisable to put them into the laying-press and screw them moderately tight. In fact, for all good work, this must be done.

In sprinkling, it is usual to tie together a number of volumes with a board on each side of the outside books, or place them in the laying-press first, with the heads upwards; then, with a large brush, similar to a painter's, dipped in whatever colour may be wished, and well beat on the press-pin over the pot till the sprinkle becomes fine, the edges are covered. The pin and brush are held sufficiently above the book, and the edge sprinkled by beating

lightly at first, and stronger as the brush becomes
less charged with colour, being careful that the
spots are as fine as possible, the sprinkle being
thereby made more beautiful.

The cleanest method, and at the same time the
surest to produce a fine sprinkle, is to use a wire
sieve and a stiff brush, something like a shoe-brush,
for convenience. The sieve should be oval in form,
with a very thick wire running round the edge
until they meet, then projecting about a foot from
the sieve so as to form a handle, the whole somewhat
resembling in shape the bat used by ball-players.
Fine brass wire is the best for the sieve. The wire
should be about one-fourth of an inch apart. After
every thing is in readiness, dip the stiff brush in the
colour and lay the sieve over the pan, and rub the
brush over it to get rid of the superfluous colour, which
will drop into the pan; then knock off all the loose
colour adhering to the sieve; then hold the sieve
over the books, and rub the brush over the wires.
lightly at first, and afterwards harder as the brush
loses the colour. The colour will descend like a fine
mist, and the effect produced upon the edge cannot
be equalled by the old method. Several colours
are sometimes used with very pleasing effect; some
of these combinations will be described, and many

others will readily occur to the workman as his taste may suggest.

COLOURS.

Of vegetable colours, and ochres, directions for mixing which have been given above, it will only be necessary to particularize the most approved and generally-used substances. The liquid ones will require a more lengthened description.

BLUE.—Indigo and Prussian blue, with whiting for lighter shades.

YELLOW.—Dutch pink, King's yellow, and yellow orpine.

BROWN.—Umber, burnt over the fire.

RED.—Vermilion; or Oxford ochre, burnt in a pan.

PINK.—Rose-pink; to make it brighter, add lake.

GREEN.—The first and second mixed to any shade.

The liquid or spirit colours will be found best for use, as the edges will not rub, which all other colours are liable to do. Some of the receipts are well known; but, it being necessary to give a faithful record of the art, the whole of the colours used and modes of preparation will be presented.

*7

BLUE.

Two ounces of the best indigo, finely powdered, mixed with a teaspoonful of spirit of salts and two ounces of best oil of vitriol. Put the whole into a bottle, and let it remain in boiling water for six or eight hours, and mix with water as wanted to the shade required.

YELLOW.

French berries, saffron, or faustic chips. Boil with a small portion of alum; strain and bottle for use.

GREEN.

The two colours above will make an excellent green used in proportions as the shade required. Another green may be made by boiling four ounces of verdigris and two ounces of cream of tartar till a good colour is produced.

ORANGE.

Two ounces of Brazil dust, one ounce of French berries, bruised, and a little alum. Boil in water and strain.

RED.

Brazil dust, half a pound; alum, two ounces, well powdered; boiled in a pint of vinegar and a pint of

water till brought down to a pint. Strain and
bottle. The red edges now in vogue are made
with vermilion, mixed with vellum-size. The better
class are scraped before they are coloured, and
afterwards they are burnished.

PURPLE.

Logwood chips, in the proportion of half a pound
to two ounces of alum, and a small piece of copperas, boiled in three pints of soft water till reduced a third, will make a good purple.

Brazil dust, submitted to the action of strong
potash water, will make a good purple for immediate use, but will not keep.

BROWN.

A quarter of a pound of logwood, and the same
quantity of French berries, boiled together. If a
darker shade is required, add a little copperas.
Plain brown edges are made with burnt umber,
in the same manner as that described for red edges.

With these colours, edges of books may be
sprinkled to almost an infinite number of patterns.
A few will be given; for, though fancy sprinkles
are seldom used where the binder can get the edges

of extra books marbled, they will be of use to those
who would find marbling a work of too great preparation and expense for a small number of books
in places where there is no marbler.

RICE MARBLE.

This pattern has been so called from the use of
rice; but linseed, or bread crumbs, will answer the
same purpose.   The rice is laid on the edge of the
book according to fancy, and the edge sprinkled
with any colour, the rice thus forming blank spaces.
The edge may be coloured previously all over, or
sprinkled with a lighter shade.

WHITE SPOT.

Take white wax and melt it in a pot; then with
a brush throw some upon the edge of the book ; when
it is set, colour the edge with a sponge.   Take the
book and give it two or three smart knocks on the
end of the press, when the wax will fly off and a
beautiful white spot remain.   This pattern may be
much varied by using two or three colours or
sprinkling the edge before the wax is thrown on,
and, after it is, again with other colours.

Whiting mixed with water to a thick consistency

will nearly answer the same purpose, and is less expensive than wax.

FANCY MARBLE.

Take a small portion of rose-pink, green, or any other vegetable colour, and well bray it on the slab with the muller, till reduced to a fine powder. Prepare a dish, or other vessel, large enough to admit the fore-edge of the book, and filled with clear water; then with the *palette-knife* mix a portion of the colours with spirits of wine, and convey with the knife some of the same to the middle of the vessel, and allow it to flow gradually on the surface of the water. The spirit of wine will cause it to spread in a diversity of pleasing forms, when the edge of the book must be dipped in the same manner as for marbling, and a very neat pattern will be produced at a trifling cost, as no more colour need be mixed than wanted at each time.

GOLD SPRINKLE.

After the edges of the book are stained with any of the colours above described, a good effect may be given by sprinkling with a gold liquid, made in the following manner:—Take a book of gold and half an ounce of honey, and rub them together in a mortar until they are very fine; then add half a pint of clear water and mix them well together. After the water clears, pour it off and put in more, till the honey is all extracted and nothing left but the gold; mix one grain of corrosive sublimate with a teaspoonful of spirits of wine, and when dissolved put the same, with a little thick gum-water, to the gold, and bottle it, always shaking it well before using. When dry, burnish the edge, and cover it with paper till the work is finished.

MARBLING.

Marbling is an art which consists in the production of certain patterns and effects by means of colours so prepared as to float upon a preparation of mucilaginous liquid, possessing certain antagonistic properties to the colours prepared for the purpose, and which colours, when so prepared, floated and formed into patterns upon the surface of the liquid, are taken off by laying thereon a piece or sheet of paper or dipping therein the smoothly-cut edges of a book.

It is a process which it is not very easy to describe; and yet, to any one beholding it for the first time, nothing appears more simple or easy of execution. Yet the difficulties are many; and the longer any one practises it, the more he will become convinced that there are many more discoveries to be made before the art can be brought to any thing like perfection or effects produced with that certainty which the workman could desire. In short, it may be said to be still in its infancy.

When the art was first discovered, and by whom, or in what city or country it was first practised, it is hardly possible to determine. It is supposed that we cannot go farther back for its origin than the beginning of the seventeenth century, and that Holland has the honour of being the birthplace of the art,—the old Dutch and some drawn and antique patterns, with stormont and other spots, being considered the most original.

Many years ago this old Dutch paper, in the size of foolscap, was imported into England, wrapped round small parcels of Dutch toys, and thus passed free of duty. When taken off, it was carefully smoothed and sold to bookbinders, commanding a high price, being only used on the better kinds of work. Indeed, so choice was it that you may still see in some old books the inside-linings made of pieces carefully joined together. Something of the art has unfortunately been lost since that time, for both the colours and the execution of some of these old specimens far surpass the best efforts of the most celebrated modern marblers.

It is proposed, however, to show, as clearly and briefly as possible, how it is done and practised at the present day by the best English workmen, and to describe the various processes in such a manner as will enable any individual possessed of a common share of understanding and discernment, to do it himself; and, where there are two ways of doing it, that will be described which experience has pronounced to be easiest and best.

In describing one pattern, that will be considered sufficient to include all of the same class, or that are done in the same manner, although different colours may be used. For instance, a brown may be described, and green, being the same in every respect as regards the mixing and working the colours, may be substituted for the brown; and so in regard to other colours.

COLOURS.

The colours required for marbling are the same as those ordinarily used for painting both in oil and distemper. They should be procured in a dry state, just as they are produced or manufactured, and ground by the marbler himself. A list is subjoined :—

REDS.

Drop Lake.
Peach-wood Lake.
Vermilion.
Rose-Pink.
Oxford Ochre, Burnt.

BLUES.

Indigo.
Chinese Blue.
Ultramarine.
Prussian Blue.

YELLOWS.

Lemon Chrome.
Dutch Pink.
Oxford Ochre, Raw.

BLACKS.

Vegetable Lamp-Black.
Drop Ivory-Black.

8

BROWN.

Turkey Umber Burnt.

ORANGE.

Orange Lead.
Orange Chrome.

WHITE.

China Clay.
Pipe-Clay.
Flake White.   .
Paris White.

DROP LAKE.

This is the most beautiful, but the most expensive,
of all the reds, and is used only for book-edges and
the most superior kinds of work.   There are different shades of this colour, viz. : — scarlet, crim-
son, and purple.   The scarlet is the most expensive, and looks the best on edges, possessing a
brilliancy which no other colour will produce ; but
there is a great quantity of a very inferior kind of
drop lake about, which is of no use whatever to a
marbler, for, when it comes to be worked, it is found
to possess no body.

In order to ascertain whether the article about to be purchased will answer, take a piece of the colour, and, breaking it, apply the broken part to the tongue. If it adhere to the tongue, it is very doubtful whether it will do; but if it hold up the moisture without any inclination to adhere, it may be tried with better expectations. This colour is sold in the form of small cones or drops, from which it derives its name, and is a preparation of cochineal; therefore the value of it depends much upon the price of that article.

VERMILION.

This colour is but little used, on account of its great specific gravity, and seldom without being combined with some other colour. It is a preparation of mercury, and, though nominally at a much lower price than lake, yet so little of it goes to a pound, it comes nearly as dear as that article.

ROSE-PINK.

This is a very useful though common colour. It is composed of chalk or whiting coloured with Brazil wood; consequently it is what is termed a fugitive colour, the pink very quickly fading on exposure to the atmosphere or to heat. When combined with indigo or a little Chinese blue it makes a good purple.

BURNT OCHRE.

This colour is obtained in its native state from pits dug in the earth in the neighbourhood of Oxford; hence, it is called Oxford ochre, and sometimes stone ochre. It is in fact a kind of clay, and when made red-hot turns to a kind of red colour. It is one of the most useful colours, and, as the price is low, is extensively used. With the addition of a little black it makes a good brown; with a little blue or indigo it makes a good olive; or it is a good colour used by itself, and is not liable to change.

WOOD LAKE.

This is a preparation of peach-wood, and has only been introduced of late years to the notice of marblers. It is manufactured at Birmingham. This colour is an exception to the rule, as it is sold in the pulp or damp state, and may be mixed and even used without grinding, being made almost exclusively for marbling. It is the best red that can be used for general purposes, and for appearance comes next to the drop lake.

CHINESE BLUE.

This is a very beautiful but not a very durable colour. It is, however, an almost indispensable one to the marbler, as it will produce nearly every shade of blue by the addition of certain proportions of white. This colour requires to be particularly well ground, as indeed do all the blues. It is also sold at some places in the pulp or damp state. There are some very good damp blues made.

INDIGO.

This colour is a most valuable article, and cannot be dispensed with under any consideration. It is too well known to require describing. Though not a bright colour, it is one of the most durable, and for mixing and producing greens and purples of a permanent kind is invaluable. Neither can a good black be made without it. Care should, however, be taken to procure it of the best quality.

ULTRAMARINE.

This is a very beautiful colour, but must be used very sparingly, as it will not glaze or take any kind of polish, and is always inclined to rub off. The kinds now in general use are the French and Ger-
8*

man, the genuine article being far too high in price
for this kind of work.

PRUSSIAN BLUE.

This colour has been of late almost entirely
superseded by the Chinese blue, which is a much
brighter colour, Prussian blue being darker and
heavier looking, and is a very bad colour for
glazing.

DUTCH PINK.

This is a common but very useful colour. It is a
preparation of whiting and quercitron bark, and is
used in making greens, no other colour answering
the purpose so well. It is also very useful in mixing with chrome to produce the various shades of
yellow required.

CHROME.

This is of various shades, varying from a light
lemon colour to a deep orange approaching to a
red. It is a useful colour; but, unless you get it
genuine, it is very difficult to get it to work
properly.

RAW OCHRE,

Or Oxford ochre in its native state. This may
be used in certain proportions for making olive

tints combined with Dutch pink and blue or black. It is also of use in small quantities to mix with yellow when it is inclined to run off, this colour being of a very adhesive nature.

DROP IVORY-BLACK.

This colour cannot be well used alone. It may, therefore, be called only an auxiliary to others.

VEGETABLE-BLACK.

This is a superior kind of lamp-black, but prepared from vegetable instead of animal matter. It is surprisingly light, and cannot be used alone, and will not produce a black for marbling except in combination with double its weight of good Indigo.

TURKEY UMBER, BURNT.

This colour produces a very good brown, but it is not required if you have the burnt Oxford ochre, as, with the aid of that colour and a little indigo and black, any shade of brown may be produced.

ORANGE LEAD.

This is a very heavy colour, and is but little used, except for the edges of account books.

WHITE.

For this an article called China clay is used; also, for some purposes, the common pipe-clay.

GUM.

Of all the varieties of gum, there is but one that is of any use to the marbler, and that is called gum-tragacanth or gum-dragon. Too much care cannot be exercised in the choice of this article, as much of the excellence of the work depends upon it. It should be large, white, and flaky. Occasionally there will be found some very good in small white flakes; but let that in dark brown lumps be rejected at once, no matter at what price it may be offered. If used at all, it would only do for the most common kind of work; but there is, in reality, no saving in an inferior article, as one pound of a really good sort will go as far as two of a bad, and produce a far more satis-factory result. Good gum ought to dissolve in cold water; it requires at least forty-eight hours soaking, being well stirred about at intervals; but some gums take longer to dissolve. Good gum will produce a smooth surface, but bad gum will often yield a rough one, which is inimical to the purpose. Again, some will give a smooth surface, and yet possess no strength; the colours will flow well upon it and form properly, and, when the paper is taken off, will look, at first, very beautiful, but upon looking at it five or ten minutes after it has been hung up, the colours will be found running off, causing indescribable annoyance and mortification.

DIRECTIONS FOR PREPARING THE GUM.

Procure a large earthen pan, glazed on the inside, capable of containing from eight to twelve gallons of water. Put therein one pound of gum-tragacanth, and on it pour about two gallons of soft water. Stir it every few hours with a clean birch broom kept expressly for the purpose, breaking the lumps and adding more water as it thickens or absorbs that previously put in. In about forty-eight hours you may venture to use it; but seventy-two hours would be better. Some gum is all the better for a longer period, as, although a considerable portion of the gum may be dissolved, yet the best properties of it are not extracted till the whole is dissolved. It must be strained through a fine hair sieve before using, and if any lumps remain, put them back into the pan until they are all dissolved.

OF LINSEED.

It is possible to marble some patterns on mucilage of linseed, but it is a very objectionable
vehicle to work upon, and can never be made
to produce a satisfactory result. It is made either
by boiling one quart of linseed in six or eight
gallons of water, or by pouring the boiling water
upon the linseed and stirring it until it extracts
the mucilaginous properties of the seed; but it
very soon decomposes or turns to water

CARRAGEEN, OR IRISH MOSS.

This is an article used by some, and can be
dispensed with altogether: it is not a necessary
article. When used, it should be picked (the white
being the best) and well washed; then set it to
simmer in a gentle heat for an hour or two,
strain it through a fine hair sieve, and it will be
ready for use ; but it will require a portion of
the solution of gum-tragacanth to be able to do
much with it.

FLEA-SEED.

This is an article but little known except to
those who have occasion to use it. It is a small,
brown, hard seed, in size, shape, and colour closely

resembling the annoying little insect whose name it
bears, and from which it may possibly derive its
appellation. It produces a very strong and powerful mucilage — far stronger than that which can
be obtained from linseed; and what enhances
its value is that it will not so soon lose its strength
or turn to water, but will keep several days. It
is a great assistant, mixed with gum, in the making
of French and Spanish marbles, but is a total
enemy to nonpareil and drawn patterns.

To prepare it, put a quarter of a pound of the
seed into a pan, pour upon it a gallon of boiling
water, keep it well stirred for ten minutes, and let
it stand for half an hour; then stir it again for ten
minutes more, and in another half-hour add another
gallon of boiling water, stirring it as before, at
intervals, for one hour; after which let it remain,
and the seed will settle at the bottom of the pan.
When cold, pour off the top for use, and the seed
will bear more boiling water, though not so much as
at first. Sometimes the seed will yield a third
extract; but this must be determined by your judgment, as the seed, when exhausted, will lose its
viscid property, and must then be thrown away.
The seed should never be stirred up after it has

cooled, for it will settle without being again heated
or having more boiling water added to it.

OX-GALL.

The surest way of obtaining this article genuine
is by procuring it in the bladder as it is taken
from the animal, if you are acquainted with any
butcher upon whom you can depend. The gall
from some animals is very thick, but will, after
keeping some time, get thin, without at all losing
its properties; in fact, gall is all the better for
being kept, and is none the worse for a strong
smell.

WATER.

Soft or rain water, when it can be procured,
is the best adapted for all the preparations in
marbling.

OF THE PREPARATIONS OR VEHICLES REQUIRED FOR MARBLING UPON.

For Spanish, French, Italian, West End, and
British patterns, there will be required a mixture
of gum-tragacanth and the mucilage of flea-seed,
in the proportions of one quart of the latter to two
gallons of the former. Beat them well up together
till they are thoroughly mixed or incorporated with

each other, strain it through a fine hair sieve into the trough, and it will be fit for use.

For Dutch, nonpareil, curls, antiques, and, in short, all patterns which require to be formed with any kind of instrument on the preparation in the trough, use nothing but the pure solution of the gum-tragacanth ; in fact, you may marble all the patterns on this alone, so that if there be any difficulty in procuring the other articles, and you can procure good gum, you may do any or all of the patterns upon it, although some of them are improved by the addition of the mucilage of the flea-seed.

As some gum is stronger than other, it is hardly prudent or possible to give any exact weight of gum to any certain quantity of water. Practice and your own judgment must determine this. Besides, if the gum be not sufficiently soaked or beaten up, it will not yield so much or so good size as it would were it in its right state. The following will give some idea to guide in the matter :—If, on skimming the surface and sprinkling on the colours, they lose their shape and appear to turn round on the solution, especially in the corners of the trough, it is a sign that it is too thin ; if, on the other hand, on skimming there is a great resistance when the skim-

9

mer is drawn along, and, upon sprinkling on the
colours, they crack, and are a long while spreading
out, it is a sign it is too thick; but a little practice
will soon enable the learner to form a correct judgment in this matter.

OF GRINDING THE COLOURS.

On this head you must be very particular indeed;
for, if the colours are not finely or properly ground,
it cannot be expected that the work will look well.
When a large quantity is required, a colour-mill is
the most advantageous method; but if on a small
scale, or for edges, the ordinary stone and muller
will be best adapted for the purpose. Indeed, all
colours required for edges ought to be most particularly well ground upon a slab, with a muller,
the mill not grinding so finely as by this method.

The colours must all be ground with a preparation
of beeswax, in the average proportion of one ounce
of the prepared beeswax to one pound of colour.
Blues and greens require rather more. This will
prevent the colour rubbing off on the hand, and will
make it burnish or glaze easily.

DIRECTIONS FOR PREPARING THE WAX FOR GRINDING.

To attempt to grind beeswax in its native state would be a fruitless task, as it would stick to the stones and not unite with the other ingredients. To obviate this, prepare it in the following manner: Take of the very best beeswax two pounds, put it in an earthen pipkin, and with it a quarter of a pound of the very best curd-soap cut into small or thin pieces; place it in a moderate heat, and when both soap and wax are quite dissolved, (but be sure they are not boiling,) put the pipkin containing the hot liquid upon a table, take in one hand a pot of cold water, and, gently stirring the melted wax with the other, pour in the water, a little at a time, keeping it constantly stirred, and it will gradually thicken, until at last it can hardly be stirred at all. Care must be taken not to have it too hot when the water is poured in, as there is danger of it flying out of the pipkin and scalding the workman. If properly mixed, when cool, it can be pulverized between the finger and thumb; and in this state it will mix or grind with the colour easily, but ought to be rubbed or worked in with the dry colour before wetting it for grinding.

TROUGHS.

The troughs should be made of wood, perfectly flat and smooth at the bottom, and of sufficient thickness to keep them from warping. They should be about two and a half inches deep inside, and about two inches larger than the sheet of paper you intend marbling, or your edges will be imperfect. There should be about three inches parted off on the right-hand side by a sloping partition, which should be about an eighth of an inch below the sides, that the waste may be skimmed over it without running it over the top. The whole should be perfectly level and true; and, if the joints are stopped with white lead, be sure it is quite dry and hard, or it will entirely spoil the solution, and will fill the pattern with white.

FRENCH OR SHELL MARBLE.

To commence with the easiest and most common kinds of marbled papers :—the colours being properly ground, and the trough placed on a level table or fixed bench of convenient height, with some feet of spare room on each side, place the pots containing the colours on the right-hand side, and the paper or books to be marbled on the left. Let there be a

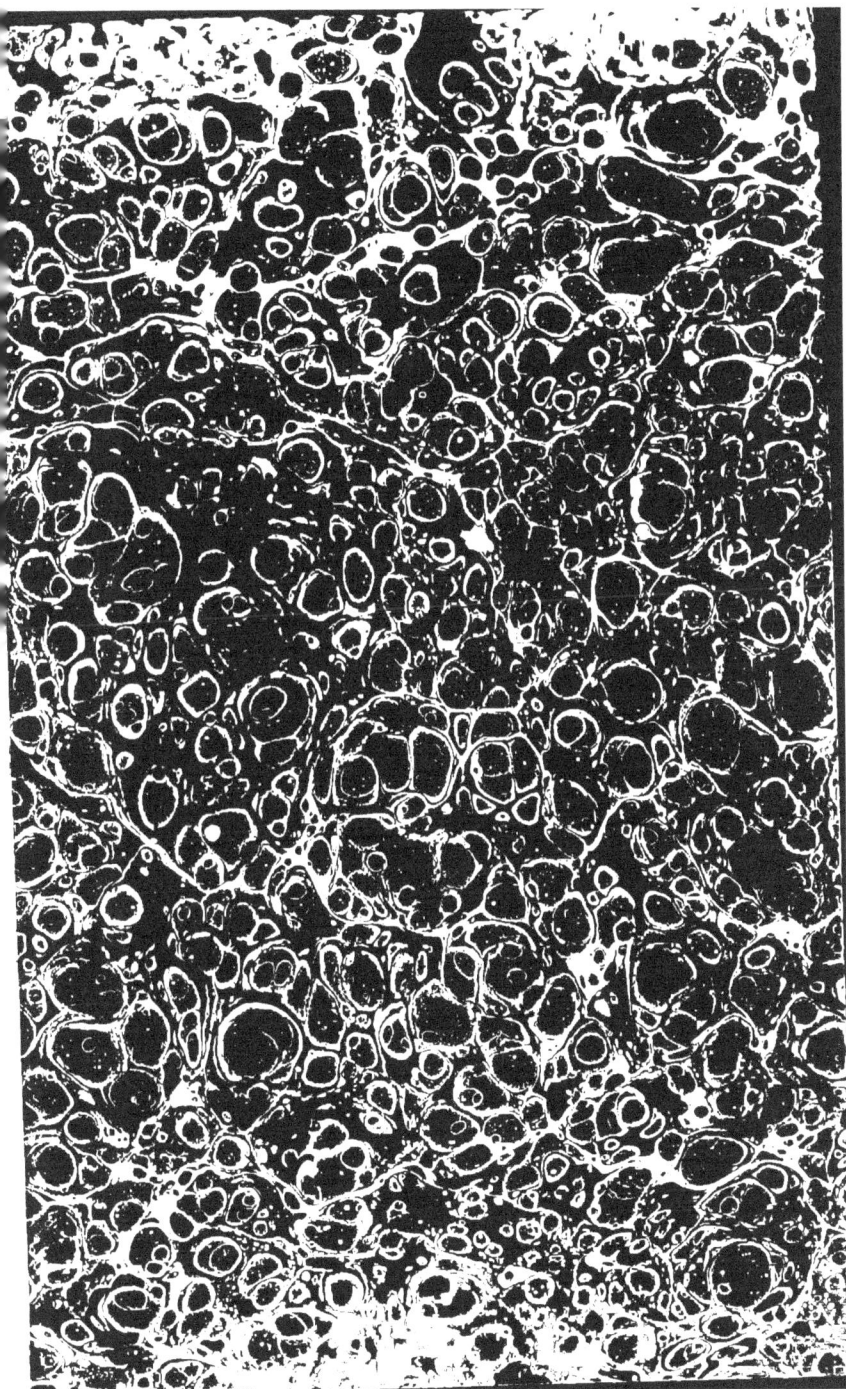

small brush in each of the pots of vein-colours, and a larger one in the last or body-colour. Have a small iron rod or bar about twelve or fourteen inches long, placed so that you may be able to take it up when required with the left hand. Fill the trough to about one-half or three-quarters of an inch from the top with the solution of gum-tragacanth and flea-seed, as previously described, and proceed to mix the colours.

For convenience of reference, the various patterns described and processes employed will be numbered.

No. 1. LARGE BROWN FRENCH OR SHELL, WITH THREE VEINS, VIZ. : RED, YELLOW, AND BLACK.

Mix together ox-gall and water in the proportion of one-eighth of the former to seven-eighths of the latter. Mix the vein-colours with this mixture, putting in a little at a time, and gently stirring it about with the brush (but be careful not to make it froth by too rapid stirring) until you arrive at the proper consistence, which must be ascertained by sprinkling a little colour on the solution in the trough. If the colour sinks, and does not spread out, add a little neat-gall; but, should it spread too far and open too much, mix a little more colour with water only, and put it to that which spreads too much.

9*

The brown will require more gall, less water, and a few drops of the very best olive-oil, which will cause it to form itself into rings or shells as it falls on the solution in the trough. This colour will require to be thicker than the vein-colours, and, when thrown or sprinkled, should drive or force the other colours into the form of veins. By increasing the quantity of gall in the last colour, it will bring the veins to almost any degree of fineness; but there is a point beyond which it is not advisable to go. If the brown does not shell enough, but forms in holes, add a few more drops of oil, and well mix it; but if there be too much oil it will spoil the effect of the shell altogether, which cannot be counteracted in any other way than by mixing some more colour without any oil, and adding it thereto.

Having, then, all in readiness, first skim the surface of the solution lightly all over, and immediately (for when you begin it is necessary to move quickly till all the colours are on) sprinkle on the colours, beginning with the red, next yellow, thirdly, black; then with the principal or body-colour go well and equally all over, taking care to throw as much colour on one part of the surface as another; then take up a sheet of paper by the two opposite corners, and let the corner between the finger and thumb of the right hand touch the surface first, while with the left you let the paper gradually descend, till it lies flat upon the liquid. If it is let down too quickly, or the paper gets rumpled, so as to allow the air to get under it, white blotches will appear when it is taken out of the trough; and if the paper be allowed to lie long enough upon the size to draw out the blisters, still the marks will show.

In order to take the paper out, lay a lath or thin stick across the centre of the paper as it lies in the trough; let it be long enough for the ends to rest upon the edges of the trough; then take hold of the paper by the two parallel corners, lay it back over the stick, lift it out of the trough by the stick, in the same manner as it might hang across a line, and place it on a rack to dry.

No. 2.—SMALL BROWN FRENCH.

This pattern is produced with precisely the same colours as No. 1, by using the iron rod previously described. It is held in the left hand, and the brush knocked against it, which causes the colour to fall in small spots, and reproduces the No. 1 pattern, as it were, in miniature.

No. 3.—BROWN FRENCH, WITH LIGHT SPOT.

This pattern has but two vein-colours—the red and the black. These are mixed with the mixture of gall and water, as described for the veins of No. 1. It has also two other colours. The brown is mixed in a similar manner to the brown for No. 1, but not quite so much gall and oil, to allow for the other colour flowing out upon it; and the last, or light spot, is composed of raw or un-burnt Oxford ochre, and is mixed with gall, water, a few drops of olive-oil, and a portion of spirits of turpentine.

No. 4.—SMALL YELLOW SHELL.

This is done in the same manner as No. 2 as regards the mixing and working, the only difference being in the body-colour.

No. 5.—BROWN AND PURPLE SHELL.

This pattern has three veins and two French colours, or colours that have been mixed as French, —that is, with oil in them,—the last of which, in this instance, is the purple. Being mixed with a little more both of the gall and oil than the other, in order to make it flow out, over, and drive up the other colours, a marbler will be able, if he follows these instructions, to imitate any French pattern, whether there be more or less colours in them.

No. 6.—BLUE STORMONT

Is an old pattern, but well worthy of being revived. Though apparently very simple and easy of execution, it is nevertheless very difficult to keep in order, in consequence of the speedy evaporation and the chemical changes which are continually taking place among the ingredients with which it is mixed. It requires great quickness and acute observation on the part of the workman.

There is but one vein-colour, (red,) and the ground or body-colour is blue. The same preparation of gum and flea-seed is used for this as for the French marble. Mix the red for vein, as usual, with gall and water. The other colour must consist of good indigo alone, without which the proper effect cannot be produced The indigo being ground, as before directed in the instructions for grinding the colours, proceed to mix the indigo with gall, water, and spirits of turpentine, — of which last ingredient it will require a considerable proportion, in order to make it break full of little holes. The acme of this pattern is to make it look like fine network. Sometimes it will happen that at first mixing it will not work, but after standing a day or two it will work well, while at other times it will work immediately. If the holes come too large from an excess of turpentine, (for they will sometimes come too large from not having enough,) add a little more gall and some fresh indigo, putting in a few drops of alum-water; but be very careful of this; for, if there be too much, it will make the colour thick and clotted: in which case have recourse to a little of the solution of potash; but it is best, if possible, to do without either of them.

No. 7.—LIGHT ITALIAN.

A very pretty though simple pattern, but requires great cleanliness of working to turn it out well. The colours being ground as before directed, proceed to mix them with gall and water only, as though they were for veins. The last colour is white; this requires a greater proportion of gall than the other colours, and a larger brush, as in the French patterns.

After skimming the size, proceed by beating or knocking on the colours,—viz.: red, green, and black, as in small French, taking especial care to have the rings of the brushes free from any accumulation of colour, or they will cause large spots or

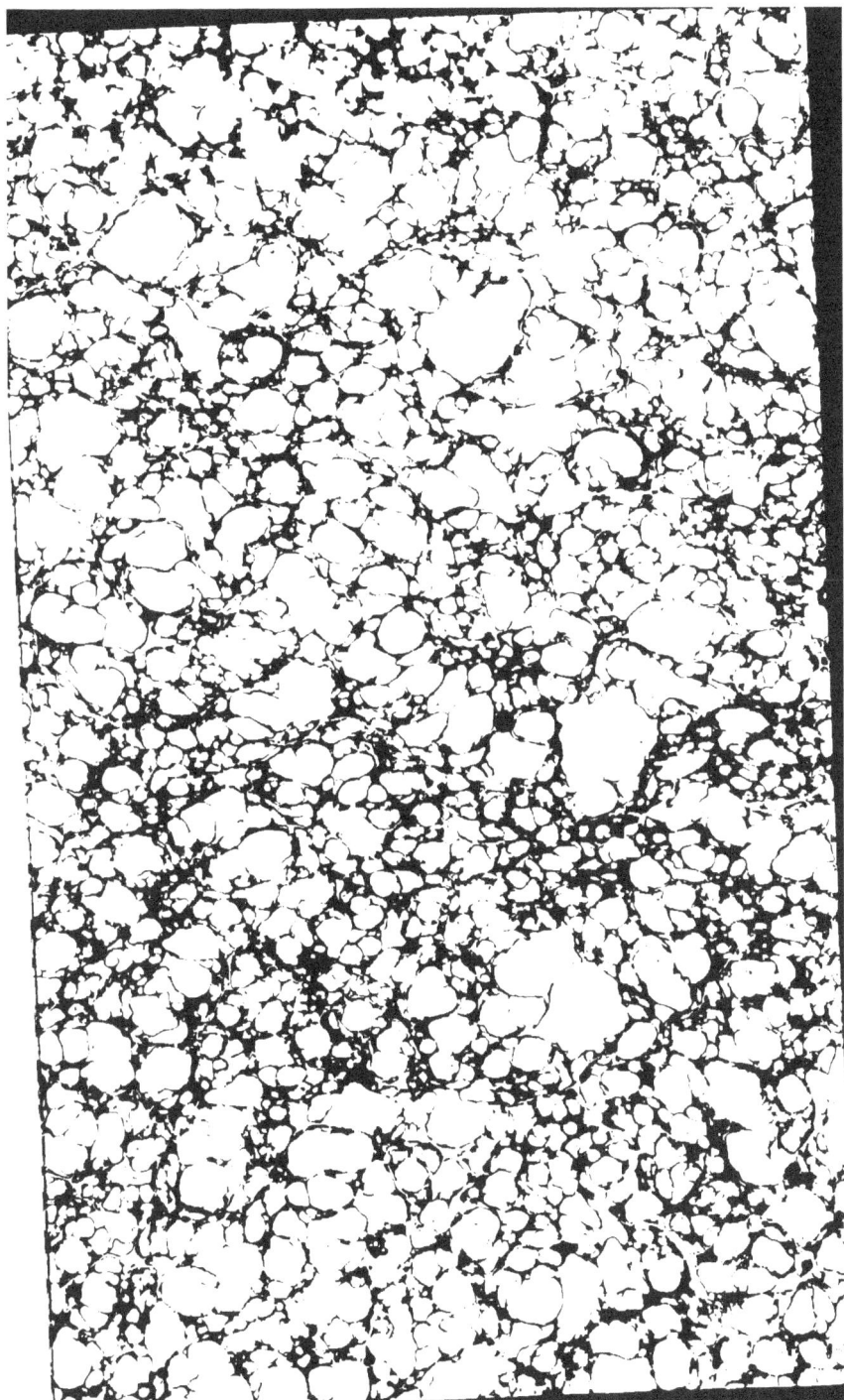

blotches, which will spoil the appearance of the work. One difference between this and the small French is that there is no oil used in any of the colours.

Another method is to use a mixture of weak gall and water instead of the white colour, and which must be firmly knocked or beaten on, proportioned by the judgment of the marbler. This method is preferable to the former for edges, and will answer quite as well for paper.

No. 8.—SMALL GREEN ITALIAN.

A very neat pattern, may be made of one colour only, which must be mixed with gall and water sufficiently strong to cover the whole surface of the solution on the trough; after which, beat on the white, or gall and water, as before. The same size, or preparation of gum and flea-seed, will do for this as for the previous marbles; it must, however, be kept clean, to make the work look nice and bright.

No. 9.—WEST END, (BROWN, WITH LIGHT SPOT.)

This pattern consists of two prominent colours besides the veins; one of these is dark and dotted all over with small white spots; the other, which is the last or top colour, is light, and is made by taking

a portion of the darker colour and mixing a quantity
ot white with it, sufficient to bring it to the desired
tint.   Mix the colours for veins in the ordinary way,
viz. : with the usual proportions of gall and water ;
then mix the brown with a larger proportion of gall,
and sprinkle it on as full as to drive the other colours
into veins ; then take the white, or gall and water,
as in Italian, and beat it finely and equally all over,
but not so much as for the Italian pattern.   Lastly,
take the light or top colour, which will require to be
stronger in gall than any of the others, and must be
sprinkled lightly and evenly over the whole ; lay on
the paper as quickly as possible.

This pattern is known by the name of West End,
and is in every respect similar to the Spanish in the
working, only it is not shaded.

No. 10.—WEST END, (GREEN, WITH LIGHT SPOT.)

An excellent pattern may be made similar to
No. 9 in all the details of mixing, working, and putting on the colours, the only difference being in the
colours, which may be made of two shades of green
or olive, and the veins red, yellow, and blue.

No. 11.—CURL.

The pattern called French Curl, after the description of the French marble (see No. 1) will not require much explanation, the only difference in the working being, that there must not be any of the preparation of the flea-seed with the gum; but it must be done on the solution of the gum alone, without any admixture. It will also require a frame with as many pegs as you may require curls on the paper; these pegs must be about three inches long, and about the thickness of a stout goose-quill, tapering toward a point. Throw on the colours the same as for No. 1 large French; take the frame of pegs, and, holding it with both hands, put the pegs down to the bottom of the trough, give it a slight rotary motion, then lift it out quickly, so that no drops fall from the pegs into the trough, and lay on the paper as usual, taking care to lay it down straight and even, or the whole pattern will be askew.

No. 12.—BROWN CURL.

A pattern of curl may be made of one colour only, mixed with the same ingredients as the ordinary French; it is the easiest of the two to make.

10

No. 13.—RED CURL.

A curl pattern may be made of the same colours used for nonpareil, only the colours and gum are both used rather thicker than for the French curl, and the colours must have no oil in them.

SPANISH.

This marble is distinguished from all others by having a series of light and dark shades traversing the whole extent of the sheet of paper in a diagonal direction. And, as it is the design of this work to simplify as much as possible, the marbler will bear in mind that all the plain Spanish patterns may be worked and managed without the aid of any other agents than ox-gall and water, of course presuming that the colours are ground and prepared as before directed.

No. 14.—OLIVE, OR LIGHT GREEN, SPANISH.

One of the most simple and easy patterns is called Olive Spanish, with red and blue veins. The veins are mixed with gall and water, as in the previous kinds of marbling, till they are brought to the proper consistence; and, as it is not possible to state any given measure for proportioning the gall and

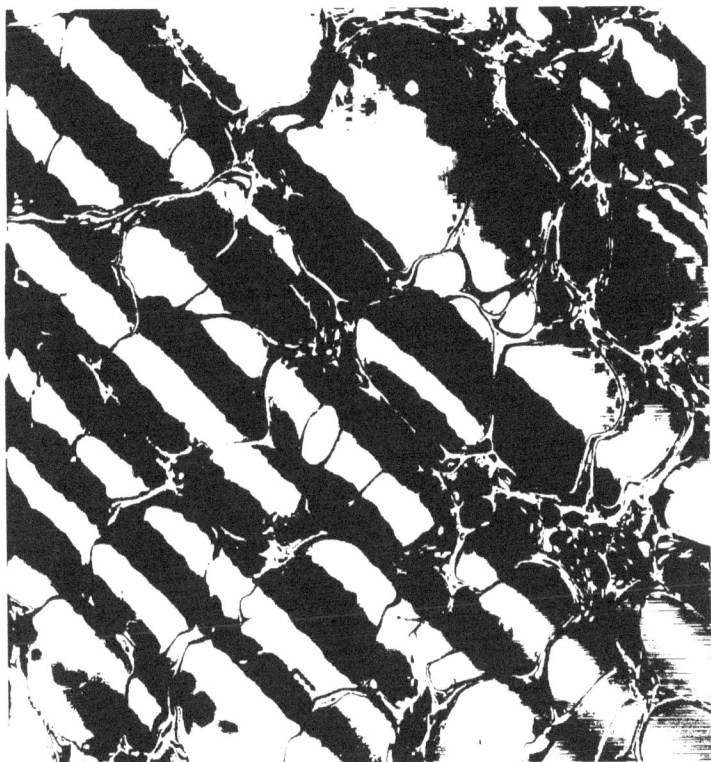

water exactly, some gall being stronger than other, that must be determined by observing the effect produced in the colours as they are tried on the solution. But each successive colour requires more gall than the one which preceded it, and the principal or body-colour requires to be both thicker in itself and stronger in gall than any of the others. This rule is almost without an exception.

Having, therefore, mixed and prepared the colours,—having the preparation of gum and flea-seed in the trough,—proceed to throw on, first the red, then the blue, and lastly, with a large brush full of colour, the olive; beginning at the left-hand corner of the trough, farthest from you, and working down and up closely all over, taking care not to go twice over the same place, or you will produce rings by the falling of one spot upon another, which is considered objectionable. It cannot, however, be entirely avoided. Now take up the paper by the two opposite corners, and, holding it as nearly upright as possible, yet with a degree of ease and looseness only to be attained by practice, let the corner in the right hand gently touch the colour on the trough, while, at the same time, you shake or move it to and fro by a regular motion, at the same time, with the left hand, letting the sheet regularly and gradually descend till it lies flat upon the surface of the solution. Practice will be required before the stripes or shades will be produced with certainty and regularity. We will next take a pattern with three veins.

No. 15.—BLUE OR SLATE SPANISH.

This is performed in a similar manner to the one just described. First, throw on red, next yellow, thirdly Blue, and lastly the slate, or body-colour, which is composed of indigo, Chinese blue, and a portion of white. We now advance a step further and take up a pattern with four veins.

No. 16.—BROWN SPANISH.

This is a well-known pattern. Perhaps as much or more of it has been made than of any other, and it always will be a standing pattern. Proceed in the same manner as before, throwing on first, the red; then yellow; thirdly, blue; fourthly, black; and lastly, the brown, which should be composed of good burnt ochre, darkened with a little black.

No. 17.—DOUBLE BROWN SPANISH.

This pattern has four colours for veins and two body-colours, the last or top colour being a dilution of the other with white. The veins are thrown on in the following order :—first, red; then black; next yellow, (some work the yellow before the black;) fourthly, green; then the brown, which must not be quite so powerful or put on quite so heavy as for brown Spanish, and on this sprinkle the light or top colour, which requires to be stronger in gall than the others.

No. 18.—FANCY SPANISH.

The pattern so designated has something of the appearance of a Spanish being worked over an Italian. It requires seven colours and brushes to execute this pattern, although it may be made of less. Commence, as usual, with red first; then black; thirdly, yellow; fourthly, blue; fifthly, green. These being all thrown or sprinkled on, next throw on the white, by using the iron rod, as for West End or Italian, and beat or knock it on very firmly all over these colours, but not so much as you would do for Italian; and lastly, the principal or body-colour,—say dark olive-green.

10*

Shade it by shaking or waving the paper in the same way as for other Spanish.

No. 19.—FANCY SPANISH.

Another compound or fancy Spanish pattern is made by introducing a small French pattern instead of veins. In doing this, be careful not to have so much gall or oil in the colours as though you were going to make French only, and the top or body-colour will require more gall than any of the plain patterns in order to make it work over the French colour.

Beautiful effects may be produced by folding the paper in squares or bending the sheets in various parts before shading, some of which cause the shades to assume an undulating appearance, as though it had been watered like silk.

No. 20.—DRAG OR EXTRA SPANISH.

To do which you must have a trough twice the length of the sheet of paper; as, in order to produce the elongated form of spots, you will have to drag or push it from one end of the trough to the other in the course of laying down the sheet of paper. The colours and preparation are the same for this as for the other Spanish, only the colours are used

considerably thinner, as they would get so thick upon the paper, from one sheet being drawn over and taking up a surface of colour usually allowed for two, that it would peel and crumble off and not burnish.

No. 21.—NONPAREIL OR COMB.

We now come to this well-known and very popular pattern, which has had a most extraordinary run, and which some people hardly seem tired of, although it has become so common of late as to be used on almost every kind of work.

For this description of marbling use the solution of gum alone in the trough. Mix the colours with gall and water, taking particular care to avoid all oil and grease of every description; but the colours will require to be thicker, and more colour thrown on, than for Spanish, with the exception of the last, which will not require to be so heavily thrown on as the last Spanish colour. Let all the colours be thrown on in about equal proportions. In commencing, proceed as usual:—first, skim the surface of the solution, and immediately follow with the red so as to well cover the whole surface of the solution; then black; next, orange or yellow; fourthly, blue; and, lastly, the top colour, of whatever shade it may be required. Now take the peg-rake, which must be as long as the trough from right to left, and which consists of a piece of wood having pegs inserted about an inch and a half apart and about three inches long, tapering towards the point, and having the appearance of the head of a rake. Pass this once up and down through the colour from front to back, taking especial care that when you draw it back the teeth come exactly between where they went up. Having raked the colour into the proper form, take the comb, which must reach the whole width of the trough from front to back, and draw it steadily through the colour, and the pattern is ready for the laying on of the paper, which must be done with a steady hand, or there will be shades in it.

No. 22.—RAKED NONPAREIL.

A very good pattern is made by following the directions for No. 21 until the colours are properly raked, then beat a little white evenly over it, and it is ready for the paper.

No. 23.—NONPAREIL, (REVERSED.)

Another pattern is made by precisely the same process as No. 21, till the colours have been raked with the peg; then take the comb, which should be a much larger one, and draw it through the colour from left to right, then immediately reverse it and draw it back again from right to left, and the desired effect will be produced.

No. 24.—ANTIQUE.

The antique marble is executed thus: after the three first colours have been thrown on, namely, red, black, and yellow, rake it once up and down with the peg-rake, after which proceed to throw on the green, follow with the pink spot, and lastly, beat or knock on small white spots. Some antique patterns are made with a blue or other coloured spot, in lieu of the pink here described, but the process is the same.

No. 25.—ANTIQUE, (ZEBRA.)

This is done with colours prepared the same as for ordinary nonpareil; throw on four colours, viz.: red, black, yellow, and blue; then rake the same as for nonpareil, after which throw on a light colour for a spot; lay on the paper the same as for Spanish. Sometimes it is made without shading, and passes for another pattern.

No. 26.—WAVE.

In this pattern the colours are drawn into an
undulating form, the points of each row meeting
each other. The colours are prepared the same as
for nonpareil. The red, yellow, blue, and green
are thrown on, over which is beaten or knocked a
small white, but not too abundantly; there is now
required a kind of double rake or frame, with teeth
of stout wire about three or four inches apart, and
let the teeth of the hinder one be so adjusted as to
be exactly in the centre of the spaces left open by
the first one; the second or hindmost row of teeth
should be an inch and a half behind the former,
the two forming but one instrument. Draw this
through the colour similar to a comb, from left to
right, but with an undulating or see-saw motion,
just sufficient to make the top of the hindermost
wave catch or touch the bottom of the foremost
one, by which means it will produce a uniform
appearance all over the sheet, something in the
appearance of irregular squares.

There are some other patterns of a similar kind
made without a small white spot, and the same
design is sometimes worked upon a French marble,
but these require no additional explanation. We now
come to

No. 27.—BRITISH.

The pattern so called is by no means easy to execute, as it requires a considerable amount of judgment to maintain any thing like uniformity. Some British patterns are made with and some without veins. They require a trough double the length of the paper, as it is dragged or pushed from one end of the trough to the other in the same manner as the drag Spanish, (No. 20;) and the size or preparation must be the same as for that kind of work. A good pattern may be made of one colour,—viz.: black. The colour for this description of marbling will be all the better for being mixed and well stirred about a few days before using, so as to become mellow for working. Two jars or pots, and a large common plate, will be required. Mix the colour in one of the jars, as if for ordinary Spanish, but not with quite so much gall; then pour a little of it into the other jar, and add to it a considerable portion of gall and water, so as to make it very thin and strong; now pour a small quantity of the strong colour (about a teaspoonful) on the plate, and, taking the brush out of the thicker colour and pressing it hard on the plate, take up with it a portion of the strong colour, and proceed to sprinkle it on quickly all over the trough. The dark and light spots will fall together, intermingling with each other and producing that variegated effect which is characteristic of the pattern. Lay on the paper the same as for drag Spanish. Brown, green, and other colours, are done in the same manner; but the colours require to be mellow and the paper soft-sized, or they are apt to run off.

No. 28.—DUTCH.

The pattern now under consideration is one of the oldest and at the same time most difficult patterns, and is performed by a very different process to any of the preceding. Upon examining this pattern, it will be perceived that the colours are not scattered here and there in an indiscriminate manner, but follow each other, in a kind of regular succession, in à diagonal direction across the sheet, red being the preponderating colour. In order to make this well, the colours must be particularly well ground, and of the first quality. They ought to be mixed a few days before using. It will be useless to expect a satisfactory result with either inferior or badly-prepared materials.

In order to accomplish this pattern, there will be required a number of little tins or pots, an inch and a half wide and about the same, or two inches, in depth.

It will also require two frames the size of the paper, with wooden pegs in them, slightly tapering, about a quarter of an inch in thickness, and fixed about three inches apart, at regular distances, over the whole extent of the space required. The colours will be all the better for this class of work by the addition of a little spirits of wine. With this exception, the colours will not require any different treatment from the nonpareil.

Mix each of the colours in a large jug, having a spout, so that you may be able to pour them out into the small tins before mentioned. The colours required will be red, yellow, green, blue, and white. The two frames of pegs must be made exactly alike. One ought to be an exact duplicate of the other.

Having mixed the colours, and tried them by dropping a little of each on the solution in the trough, proceed to fill as many of the little pots with colour as there are pegs on the frame, and arrange them about three inches apart, so that the pegs in the frames may drop into the centre of each pot, and, when lifted out, (which will require to be done with great caution,) will convey one large drop of colour on each peg, with which the surface of the size is to be gently and evenly touched, taking care not to put

11

them in too deep, but at the same time being quite
sure they all do touch the size. The tins or pots of
colour must be arranged as in the following diagram,
about three inches apart:—

```
G   Y   G   Y   G   Y   G
Y   B   Y   B   Y   B   Y
G   Y   G   Y   G   Y   G
Y   B   Y   B   Y   B   Y
G   Y   G   Y   G   Y   G
```

G standing for green, Y for yellow, and B for
blue. Then fill the same number of tins or pots
with white, which must be composed of pipe-clay
ground and prepared as the other colours, and
arrange them in precisely the same manner, using
the second or duplicate frame of pegs to these.

Having arranged all these, commence operations
by first skimming the size, (which must consist of
gum-tragacanth alone,) and then well cover the
whole surface with red, which must be thrown on
plentifully with a brush. Then carefully lift the
first frame standing in the pots of the three colours,
giving it a slight rotary motion, so as to stir the
colours, which soon settle, being careful not to
upset them. Let one drop from each peg touch
the surface of the red upon the size, then quickly

take the one with the white and drop that just in
the centre of the spots already placed on the
trough; next take a rounded piece of tapering
wood, (a brush handle is as good a thing as any,)
and pass it up and down through the colours as
they are now disposed in the trough, from front
to back, at regular distances, till the whole extent
of the trough has been gone over; then pass the
comb through it from left to right, and lay on the
paper.

As soon as you have hung it up, pour over it,
from a jug with a spout, about a pint of clear
water, to wash off the loose colour and gum and
make it look clean and bright, after which, when
dry, it will require sizing before it can be burnished.

When curls are required, it will be necessary to
have a third frame, with as many pegs as you may
require curls upon the sheet of paper.

No. 29.—ANTIQUE DUTCH

Is done in a different manner to any of the processes hitherto described. The colours used for
this kind of work must be of first-rate quality,
and must be ground with spirits of wine or extra
strong gin, and mixed up with the same and a little

gall, just sufficient to make them float and spread
to the extent required. Instead of brushes, have
a tapering piece of wood, about the thickness of a
little finger, in each pot of colour, (small pots will
do, capable of holding about a tea-cup full.) The
colours required are red, orange, blue, and green.
The red must be the best scarlet lake; the orange,
orange lead; the blue, ultramarine and indigo; and
the green, indigo and Dutch pink. These must be
ground and mixed, as before directed, to the consistence of cream. The lake should be ground one
day and the other colours a few days before using,
and kept moist. The gum will require to be used
thicker for this work than for any other. Having
every thing in readiness, take a pot of colour in the
left hand, and with the right proceed to lay on the
colour with a piece of wood or with a quill, in
sloping stripes, like those made by a school-boy in
learning to write. Commence with the red and make
two strokes almost together, leaving a small open
space, and then making two more, and so on, until
the required extent has been gone over. Next
take the orange, and make one stripe between the
two stripes of red; then proceed to fill up the wider
space with a stripe of green and a stripe of blue.
Perhaps the following may more clearly illustrate

the order in which the colours should be arranged
on the trough :—

G B R O R G B R O R G B R O R G B

As in the former instance, the initial letters
signify the colours. Draw the comb through and
the pattern is complete.

EDGES.

The patterns for edges are produced in the same
manner as those for paper; and having already
devoted so much space to this beautiful art,
hitherto confined to a few, it would be useless to
repeat the processes. Yet there are some things in
regard to edges which every good marbler should
understand. When plates are interspersed in any
book along with the letter-press, it will require particular care in marbling, or the colour and size will
run in and spoil the appearance of the plates. To
obviate this, keep the book tightly compressed, and
where the plates are at the beginning of the book
only, lay it down, when marbled, the beginning side-
upwards. For edges you may do with a smaller
trough, also a smaller quantity of colour than for
paper. The solution to work upon had better be
gum-tragacanth alone. Colours for edges will look
all the brighter by the addition of alcohol, spirits

11*

of wine, or whiskey; but they will evaporate more
quickly.   Having every thing in readiness, take the
book, or, if more than one, as many as you can conveniently manage to hold tightly, with the backs
in the right hand and the fore-edge in the left, and
let them touch the colour, the back first, allowing them gradually to descend till the whole end is
covered; but be very careful that none of the size
or colour comes over the fore-edge, which it will do
if dipped too deep, and leave a nasty unsightly
mark, and greatly disfigure the book.   In doing
the fore-edge, the beginner had better place the
volume between a pair of cutting-boards, and, having thrown out the round, turn back the boards,
and proceed as with the end; when done, wipe off
the superfluous size from the boards with a sponge,
put the boards back in their place, and let the
volume dry.

GLAZING OR BURNISHING.

The sheets of paper are burnished by a machine
constructed for the purpose.   A smoothly-faced
flint is fixed in a block of wood, in which is inserted
one end of a pole about five feet in length, the
other end being attached to and working in a
cavity in a spring-board fixed overhead, allowing

it to work backwards and forwards upon a plank hollowed out for the purpose. The paper is moved over the plank, and the friction of the flint in passing to and fro over the surface of the paper produces a high polish. Sometimes the paper is calendered by means of friction cylinders—a superior method.

COMBS.

These are made in various ways, some to be worked on the top of the trough and called top-combs, others to be worked by putting the points down to the bottom of the trough and called bottom-combs. The best thing for making them is of brass pin-wire. The comb for small nonpareil ought to have from twelve to fourteen teeth to the inch, for the second size eight, and for large, four.

SIZING THE PAPER.

It is sometimes necessary to size the paper after marbling. The way of making the size is as follows:—Take of the best white soap two pounds, put it in a large copper with about twenty gallons of water; when it is quite dissolved, add thereto about four pounds of the best glue, keeping the whole constantly stirred, to prevent the soap and glue from burning; when both are quite dissolved, strain it into a tub, and when cool, it is ready for use. Should it be found too thick, add more hot water. The best way of sizing is to fill a trough with the liquor and to lay the marbled surface of the paper down upon it, then hang it on the sticks to dry.

PATENT MARBLED CLOTH.

This is an article recently introduced, and in some quarters meets with considerable favour. There are as yet no manufactories of it in this country. It, however, possesses no advantages over good marbled paper, and for outsides will not compare with the *papier D'Anonay* for durability.

ADDENDA.

In taking leave of the subject of marbling, there is but little more to add. For, when the learner is master of all this book teaches, he will have attained such proficiency in the art as to require nothing further in the way of instruction. Should some new pattern come up, let him apply the principles that govern in mixing and distributing the colours, and, with the aid of his own experience, his chance of accomplishing it will be as good as any one else's. As a step to the attainment of mastery

in the art, let the workman divest himself of the
various nostrums he has been put in possession of
by interested parties, and give himself up with
assiduity to the directions here laid down.   What is
here given is the result of twenty-five years' actual
experience of C. W. Woolnough, of London, whose
marbles rank among the most beautiful productions
of the present day.   Therefore let the workman
adhere to the instructions, and ultimate success will
crown his efforts.   Should there be any difficulty in
obtaining any of the articles described, they may
be procured from Mr. Charles Williams, No. 213
Arch St., Philadelphia.   The specimens of marbled
paper accompanying these pages, illustrate the prominent classes or patterns of marbling.   They were
executed by him, and show his mastery of the art.

BURNISHING.

The edges are burnished by placing the volume
open, with the fore-edge between boards, similar to
backing-boards, in the laying-press, and screwing it
tightly therein; then with the burnisher rubbing
the edge firmly and smartly over till it presents a
uniformly bright surface, and free from any dents
or inequalities.   When the fore-edge is finished, the
volume must be taken out of the press, and the

head and tail burnished in a similar manner, the
ends of the boards resting in the groove by the
joints, the covered boards of the volume being
open. Common calf, sheep, and half-binding, may
be burnished with the boards closed, six or eight
together, but it will be necessary to delay pasting
the sides on the latter till after the operation, to
avoid the liability of tearing.

GILT EDGES.

This description of edge is the best preservative
against external injury and damp. Previous to
laying on the gold, the workman must have in
readiness the articles necessary to form the groundwork and cause the gold to adhere to the edge.
The first is a mixture of red bole or chalk and black
lead, well-ground and reduced by water to a fluid
consistence, after having added to it a few drops
of muriatic acid or vitriol. The size used by some
is made from the white of an egg in five times the
quantity of water well beaten together; but that
most generally used is made from parchment or
vellum shavings boiled in water to extract the
gluten. It is then passed through a piece of fine
muslin and set aside to cool. When cold it is very
easy to judge of its strength Some use ice in sum

mer-time to chill it, as a test of its strength. If
too strong or thick, add water, then warm it to melt
the size and allow the water to become incorporated
with it. To become a good gilder requires considerable judgment, as every variety of paper requires a different treatment. No rule can be laid
down that will answer in every case; but if the
workman will but pay attention to the directions
here given, exercise patience, and above all reflect
upon the effects of his operations, ultimate success
will be certain. English books are made from linen
rags, and the paper is sized. They gild more easily
and the edge looks better than American books.
They do not require as strong a size for gilding as
books printed on paper made from cotton. Books
printed in this country are generally made from
cotton rags. Quantities of alum and lime are employed in bleaching the pulp, to the sore annoyance
of many a gilder, who has found that a damp day
would invariably put both his skill and patience to
the test. The best qualities of American paper are
sized; the generality, however, is not. To determine whether the paper is sized or not, apply the tip
of the tongue to it; if it adhere to the tongue, it is not
sized, and will consequently require a stronger size
for gilding than if it were sized paper. The liability

of parchment size to decompose or turn to water in
hot weather can be entirely counteracted by adding
a very small portion of oxalic acid. Having every
thing in readiness, put the book in the laying-press,
between the gilding-boards, placed even with the
fore-edge of the book and with the cheeks of the
press; screw up as tightly as possible with the
press-pin.

Then commences the most difficult operation, and
one upon which the beauty of the edge almost
entirely depends—namely, that of scraping. This
is done with a steel scraper. A piece of saw-blade
answers the purpose very well. After being ground
square on the edge and rubbed perfectly smooth
upon the oil-stone, it is kept in order by a smooth
steel. The edge must be scraped perfectly smooth,
so as not to show the marks of the knife in cutting,
or of the scraper. After this is done, it must
be coloured lightly over with the bole or chalk,
rubbed immediately dry with fine clean paper
shavings. This process will have to be repeated
three times; it is then well burnished with the
agate, and, with a broad, flat camel's-hair pencil, or
piece of soft sponge, a coat of size laid evenly
on the surface.

The gold is next cut on the gold-cushion to the

size required. A slip of paper larger than the edge is drawn over the head of the workman, and by a light pressure upon the cushion the gold will attach itself to the paper; it is then turned, with the gold upwards, (care being taken to have sufficient upon the paper to cover the entire edge,) and laid upon the cheek of the press; then pass a flat camel's-hair pencil, dipped in clean water, evenly over the edge, and immediately lay on the gold by taking up the paper, turning the gold towards the edge, and presenting it with sufficient celerity not to allow the gold to be drawn from the paper in portions by the size. To do this well will require some practice and a steady hand. Should there be any breaks in the gold, other portions must be applied, and, if dry, moisten with water applied by a fine pencil, and lay on the gold.

After the edge is entirely dry, which generally happens in from one to two hours, it must be burnished. For this purpose a flat blood-stone burnisher is the best, to be afterwards followed by a flat agate. Let there be no marks of the burnisher, but spare no pains in burnishing to have the edge perfectly uniform and clear. The head and tail of the volume must be gilt with

12

the same precaution, the back towards the workman. The foregoing directions have been derived from the practical experience of Mr. James Pawson, one of the best gilders in this country.

Should the work be of such a nature that it is desirable to give it the character of the period in which the book was written, or an additional degree of beauty and elegance, this part of book-ornament may be pursued further in the manner we shall now describe.

ANTIQUE STYLE.

After the edge is finished as above directed, and before taking out of the press, ornaments, such as flowers, or designs in compartments, must be stamped upon it in the following manner. A coat of size is passed quickly over with great precaution and lightness, and only once in a place, to avoid detaching any of the gold. When dry, rub the edge as lightly as possible with palm-oil, and cover with gold of a different colour to the first; then with the tools used in gilding leather, warmed in the fire, proceed to form the various designs by firmly impressing them on the edge. The gold that has not been touched by the tools is then rubbed off with a clean cotton, and there remains only the designs the tools have imprinted, which produce a fine effect. This mode is, however, now seldom used, though almost all the books in the original binding of the sixteenth century are so executed.

GILDING UPON MARBLED EDGES.

This edge, which Dr. Dibdin, in his "Bibliographer's Decameron," calls "the very luxury, the *ne plus ultra* of the Bibliopegistic Art," is one requiring great care and expertness in the execution. The edges must be scraped before marbling. After the edges have been tastefully marbled, and not overcharged with colour, the book must be put in the press, and well burnished as before directed. The size must then be laid lightly on, to prevent unsettling the colour of the marble, by which the edge would be destroyed, and the gold immediately applied and finished off as in other edges. When dry the marble is perceived through the gold, and presents an appearance of great beauty.

GILDING ON LANDSCAPES, ETC.

When the edge is well scraped and burnished, the leaves on the fore-edge must be evenly bent in an oblique manner, and in this position confined by boards tied tightly on each side, until a subject is

painted thereon in water-colours, according to the
fancy of the operator. When perfectly dry, untie
the boards and let the leaves take their proper position. Then place the volume in the press, lay on
the size and gold, and, when dry, burnish. The
design will not be apparent when the volume is
closed, from the gold covering it; but when the
leaves are drawn out it will be perceived easily, the
gilding disappearing, and a very unique effect will
be produced. The time and labour required makes
this operation expensive, and it is consequently very
seldom performed. It is, however, considered necessary to describe the proceeding, as the taste or
wishes of some may render it necessary that the
workman should know how to operate.

After the volume is gilt, the edges must be en-
veloped in clean paper, by glueing the extremities
one upon the other, to preserve the edges from injury in the subsequent operations. This is taken
off when the volume is completed.

BLACK EDGES.

Books of devotion are generally bound in black leather, and, instead of being gilt on the edge, blacked
to correspond with the covers. It will therefore be
necessary in this place to describe the process.

Put the book in the press as for gilding, and sponge it with black ink; then take ivory-black, lamp-black, or antimony, mixed well with a little paste, and rub it on the edge with the finger or ball of the hand till it is perfectly black and a good polish produced, when it must be cleared with a brush, burnished, and cased with paper.

Coloured edges, to look well, require to be scraped in the same manner as for gilt. To lay the colour on evenly, and produce a high burnish, requires more labour than gilding. They are therefore quite as expensive. After the colouring or gilding of the edges, the next process is to attach the

REGISTER,

To do which the back, near the head, is lightly touched with glue, and one end of a piece of ribbon proportioned to the volume is affixed. The leaves are opened, and the other portion of the ribbon placed between the leaves; the portion intended to hang out at the bottom being turned back until the book is completed, to prevent its being soiled.

HEADBANDS.

The headband is an ornament in thread or silk, of different colours, placed at the head and tail of a

12*

book on the edge of the back, and serves to support
that part of the cover projecting above in consequence of the squares of the boards, giving to the
volume a more finished appearance. Thus it will be
seen that the headband must equal the square
allowed for the boards. For common work, the
headband is made of muslin pasted upon twine;
but for extra work, and volumes requiring greater
durability, it is made of thin board and parchment
pasted together and cut into strips of the breadth
required. These flat headbands produce a much
better effect than the round ones.

There are two kinds of headbands,—viz.: single
and double. For ordinary work, cloth pasted round
the band, or common thread, is used; for extra, silk
and sometimes gold and silver thread. If the volume
is small, it is placed, with the boards closed and
drawn down even with the edge, between the knees;
or, if larger, placed at the end of the laying-press,
with the fore-edge projecting towards the body of
the workwoman. (The headbands are usually worked
by females.)

SINGLE HEADBAND.

Take two lengths of thread or silk, of different
colours, threading one in a long needle, and tying

the ends of the two together. Supposing red and
white to have been taken, the white attached to the
needle, it is placed in the volume five or six leaves
from the left side, and forced out on the back immediately under the chain-stitch of the sewing, and
the thread drawn until it is stopped by the knot,
which will be hid in the sheet; the needle is then
passed a second time in or near the same place, and,
after placing the prepared band under the curl thus
made, the thread is drawn tight, so as to hold it
firm. Before placing the band, it must be bent with
the fingers to the curve of the back of the book.
The red thread is now taken with the right hand,
and, bringing it from the left to the right, crossed
above the white thread, passed under the band, and
brought round to the front again and fastened by
passing over it, in the same way, the white thread,
taking care that the bead formed by these crossings
touches the edge of the volume. In repeating thus
alternately the operation, crossing the two threads
and passing each time under the band, which is
thereby covered, it must be occasionally fastened to
the book by inserting the needle, as before directed,
once in as many places as the thickness of the book
may require, and giving it a double tack on the
right side on completing the band, fastening it on

the back with a knot. These fastenings give firmness to the headband and the exact curve of the
back. The two projecting sides of the band must
be cut off near the silk, giving the band a slight inclination upwards, to prevent the work slipping off
before covering.

DOUBLE HEADBAND.

This headband is made of silk of various colours,
and differs from the single, both in being composed
of two bands, a large and small one, and in the
manner of passing the silk. It is commenced in the
same way as the single; but, when the bands are
fastened, the smaller above the larger, the red silk
is taken with the right hand and passed above the
white, under the bottom or larger band, brought out
under the upper or small one, carried over it, brought
out again over the large band, and the bead formed, .
as above directed, near to the edge of the book.
The white silk is then passed in the same way, and
so on alternately till the whole is completed.

GOLD AND SILVER HEADBAND

Both single and double made as above, the only
difference being in the use of gold or silver thread.

Great care must be here observed in tightening the thread at the bead.

RIBBON HEADBAND.

This style varies but little from the other, the same-coloured thread being only passed several times round, instead of alternately with the other, and making the bead at each turn, taking care that the under thread is not observed, and then passing the other colour, in a similar manner, as many or more times than the former. This will produce a band—from which it is named—having the appearance of narrow ribbons of various colours. Three or more colours may be used in a pattern.

COVERING.

The skins prepared for binding are dressed in a peculiar manner. They are soft and of equal thickness throughout. The cutting out of covers is an important operation, as by attention much economy may be effected. For this purpose patterns in pasteboard of all the sizes of books should be made, and such as are required placed on the skin, turning them every way, so as to obtain the greatest number of pieces possible, allowing about an inch round for paring and turning in. Should the books be of the same size, a volume taken by the fore-edge and the boards laying open on the leather will enable the workman to judge to a nicety the most advantageous way to cut. The narrow pieces, &c. left on the sides will do for the backs and corners of half-bound work. The leather must be cut out dry, except russia, which must be well soaked with warm water, care being taken to avoid creasing. It will also require to be well rubbed out on a marble slab with the folder. If the russia is grained properly in the skin, it will not require wetting or rubbing.

Each cover must be pared round the edges with a long knife, called the paring-knife; and great care and skill are requisite in order to do it well. The French binders use a knife for this purpose somewhat similar to a chisel; and it must be confessed that their bindings surpass in this respect those of any other country. It is impossible to determine the precise point at which the paring commences. The declension is so gradual that it cannot be perceived. As an illustration of this fact, there is a specimen of Bauzonnet's in the possession of a connoisseur of this city, covered with very thick Levant morocco, with a joint of the same material, and the interior of the board lined with morocco, thus making three different pieces. And the paring is so exquisitely done that, were it not for the colours, it would be impossible to tell where they joined. The whole interior of the board is as level as a piece of polished marble.

Whatever may be the substance or material with which a book is covered, the manipulations are the same. It is well pasted over with the brush and placed on the volume in the same way, care being taken to preserve from stains those that are costly and delicate, particularly morocco and calf. The cover should be placed on a board, and the side of the skin which is to be applied to the volume pasted well and evenly upon the surface, leaving no more than what is necessary to make it adhere. The cover being then laid on a table, or clean milled board, the volume is taken in the hands, the squares at head and tail equally adjusted, and placed upon the nearest side of it, in such a position that the back of the volume, which is from the workman, will be in the middle. The far part is then brought over to the other side, and care taken not to disarrange the squares. The cover, which now projects an inch all round the volume, is drawn tightly on the back with the open hands, by turning the projecting portion of the cover outward and resting the book on the fore-edge, at the same

time working the leather in such a manner that it
will adhere closely to the sides of the raised bands
as well as to the back. A square band, with the
leather fitting closely and evenly to the back on
each side of the band, is a great point to attain,
and any thing short of it is a blur upon the binding. After the back has been sufficiently manipu-
lated, lay the cover perfectly smooth upon each
side, then open the boards and lay one upon the
paring-stone, and pass the paring-knife between
the board and the cover diagonally across the
corner of the latter, in such a manner that, when
the leather is turned over, one edge will merely
fold over the other; turn the book and operate in a
similar manner on the other corners.

The cover at the head and tail of the book must
next be turned in, by taking it by the fore-edge
and placing it upright on the table with the boards
extended, and with the hands, one on each side,
slightly forcing back the boards close to the headband, and folding the cover over and into the back
with the thumbs, drawing it in so that no wrinkle or
fold is seen. Having turned in the cover the whole
length of the boards, the volume must be turned
and operated on at the bottom in a similar manner.
The volume is then laid flat upon one side, and the

cover turned over the fore-edge of the other, the corners being set by the aid of the thumb-nail and folder as neatly as possible; the same operation is repeated upon the other side. Any derangement of the square of the boards that may have taken place in covering must also be rectified.

The setting of the headband is the next operation, which is very important to the beauty of the binding, by properly forming a sort of cap over the worked headband of the leather projecting across the back a little above a right line from the square of one board to the other. With a small smooth folder, one end a little pointed, the double fold of the leather must be rubbed together to make it adhere, and, if the boards have been cut at the corners, the hand applied thereon, and finally forcing the headband close to the leather, staying it even on the back with the finger, and forming a neat cap of the projecting part on the top of it. The folder is then applied on the edges of the boards, to give them a square appearance and make the leather adhere. One board is then thrown back, the folder placed lengthwise along the joint or groove, holding it firmly by the right hand; the board is then gently forced by the left hand until it projects slightly within or over the joint. Upon

13

this depends the freedom and squareness of the joint,—one of the most charming features of a well-bound book. After this operation has been performed upon both boards, the headbands will again require attention; and, in order to set them firmly, pass a piece of sewing-thread around the book between the back and the boards, and, after it is tied, manipulate the head as before, so as to make it perfectly square and even with the boards and back. The volume is rubbed alongside of the bands, and then set aside until nearly dry, when the thread is taken off and the boards again set in the joint.

If the book has been sewn on bands, or if the artificial bands are large, it is sometimes necessary, to make the leather adhere to the back, that the volume should be *tied up*, which is done by placing a board, longer than the book, on each side, projecting slightly over the fore-edge, and tying them tightly with a cord from end to end. Then, with a smaller cord, the leather is confined to the sides of the bands, by crossing the string. For example: suppose the book had three bands, one towards the head, one towards the tail, and the other in the middle; the book would be taken in the left hand, the head upwards, the cord by the help of a noose passed round close to the inside of the band nearest to the tail and drawn tight, then carried round again and brought close to the other side. The string, tightened, is thus crossed on the other side of the volume, and the band held between it. The cord is in like manner carried on to the second and third bands, fastened, and the whole set square with the folder. It will be best understood by the following engraving.

For morocco, and books in other substances, having but small bands, tying up is not resorted to, being generally rubbed close in with the folder, or a box stick for the purpose. Antique work having high, narrow bands, must have the leather well worked in between the bands by the hands, and then the bands must be compressed by the band-nippers. For morocco, however, where the beauty of the grain is liable to be destroyed, great care must be taken, as the slightest mark or scratch is indelible.

A few observations must not be omitted relative to morocco, velvet, silk, and coloured calf, which, from their nature, require the greatest neatness to

avoid stains and alterations in the colours. Covers
of the former description must not be drawn on too
tight or rubbed with the folder, as the grain or pattern of the material would thereby be destroyed; and
extra care must be taken with the coloured calf to
prevent damage. They must be drawn on with the
hands on each side at the same time. The table
should be covered with a marble slab, and the hands
kept perfectly clean. Silk should be prepared previously, by pasting a piece of paper thereon, and
be left to dry, so that, when pasted for covering,
the dampness will not affect its appearance. Velvet will require great care, from its peculiar texture making it necessary that it be rubbed one
way only in covering. From this cause, having
ascertained the direction of the *nap*, the back of the
book is glued and laid upon it and drawn smoothly;
then the sides are in like manner glued over,
and afterwards the edges turned in. This proceeding causes the whole to lie perfectly smooth,
which velvet would not do if drawn in a contrary
way to the grain or nap, or if the glue was applied
to the velvet.

HALF-BINDING.

Half-binding—so called from the backs and corners only being covered with leather—has come so much into vogue that it may now be said to be the favourite style of binding. This is not to be wondered at; for, while it combines economy and durability, it can also be made to exhibit a great deal of neatness. To do this, however, requires more care and skill in paring the back and corners than is generally required for full binding. The transition from the thick morocco to the paper used on the sides can be made almost imperceptible to the touch by a skilful use of the paring-knife or chisel. The general directions for covering will be sufficient for the class of work under consideration. After the back is lettered or finished, the corners may then be put on; and, after carefully marking and cutting the paper selected for the purpose, the sides should be glued carefully over and affixed to the boards, having sufficient projection to turn inside of the board far enough to be covered by the endpapers. The width of the back should be governed by the size of the volume. A narrow back gives a very meagre appearance to a book. The size of the corners should be determined by the width

13*

of the back. The end-papers are pasted down and
the work finished in the same way as will be pointed
out for binding in general. The colour of the paper
used for sides should harmonize with the colour of the
leather. The English generally prefer the inside-
paper, the edges, and the outside-paper, to match;
and it must be confessed that, when the paper is of
good quality and the edges correspond, the effect is
extremely good. The French generally use a light
tint of marble-paper for the inside, and a darker
shade for the outside. For durability as an outside-
paper, there is nothing equal to the *papier d'Anonay*,
vellum being one of its components. Of this article
there are many worthless imitations, which yet in
external appearance are well calculated to deceive.
The real article will wear as well as the morocco
used for the back and corners. The best class of
half-binding for amateurs is the Font Hill style,
half morocco, of the best quality; uncut leaves, so
as to preserve the integrity of the margin; top-edge
gilt, as a protection from dust; lined with the best
English paper; worked-silk headbands; outside-
paper to harmonize with the back; no gilding on the
back except the lettering. This style requires extra
pains in the forwarding and covering, as the slightest
defect in these particulars cannot be remedied by

the finisher. In other bindings, the brilliancy of the gilding often serves to conceal or to allure the eye from those portions of the binding that a workman would pronounce to be "botched."

Uncut books are trimmed to a general line with a large knife, similar to a butcher's-knife, previous to being glued up. They are the special favourites of book-collectors. An uncut copy of a scarce work will always command a higher price than one that has been cropped.

STATIONERY OR VELLUM BINDING.

This branch of the Art of Bookbinding, in large towns, is a distinct business, and presents some difference in the mode of proceeding in several of the manipulations required. These, as in previous parts of the work, will be minutely entered into for the instruction of the young workman, while those which are executed in the same manner as directed for printed books will be merely referred to in the order they will be required to be executed.

Stationery binding includes every description of paper-book, from the *Memorandum*, which is simply covered with marble-paper, to the most firm and elaborately bound book used in the counting-house

of the merchant and banker. Of the more simple
and common bindings, it will not be necessary to
enter into minute details, the proceedings being the
same as for others, only omitting the more expensive operations, the price allowed making it necessary to bind them in a more simple manner. The
first proceeding, should the work require it, will
be the

RULING.

This is done by a machine. Formerly it was
done by hand. After the pens are properly adjusted, the paper to be ruled is placed upon the
table in front of the ruling-machine, and the
rollers set in motion. The sheet is caught and
passed under the pens. It is then carried by
the cloth and cords and laid away to give place
to another. The most elaborate patterns can be
executed upon the ruling-machine.

Although machine-ruling has almost entirely superseded the old process of ruling by hand, yet to
some a brief description of the process may not be
unacceptable.

The paper, which is generally procured from the
wholesale stationers ruled with blue lines, must be
opened out by breaking the back of the fold, and

refolded evenly in small sections. The pattern for
the red lines being placed in front, the whole must be
knocked evenly up at the back and head, put between
boards, the top of the paper projecting, and screwed
in the laying-press. Then, with the saw, let the
marks of the red ink on the pattern be sawn across
the whole, which will denote the places for the lines
on the right-hand side pages throughout the book.
In like manner, placing the pattern on the other
side, and sawing the bottom of the paper, will the
marks of the left-hand pages be denoted. Care must
be taken to leave a larger space on the fore-edge, to
allow for cutting. Should a head-line be required,
it must be similarly marked on the fore-edge of the
paper. This done, reopen the whole of the sections, and, with a round ruler and tin pen, proceed
to rule the whole of the head-lines on one side
of the paper. This, as well as every division of
$ cts., or other distinct column, must be ruled
double, as close as possible, taking care that both
are distinct, and that they do not run into each
other. The head-line being completed on one side,
turn the whole of the paper, and operate in like
manner on the other. Then, turning the paper, so
as to have the head-lines to the left, proceed to rule
the columns marked for the *date, amount,* &c.,

taking especial care that the pen always commences
by the line at the head, and that it never en-
trenches on the space above, which would disfigure
the work.   As for the head-line, so here the whole
of one side of the paper must be completed before
the other is commenced, attention being paid to
each line being perpendicular, clear, and as even in
colour as possible.

The cut on the following page represents a
machine for printing the figures upon the head of
the pages, formerly done by the accountant with a
pen; but now no blank bindery is considered complete without a paging-machine.   These machines
are manufactured by H. Griffin, New York.   The
sheets are paged by this machine before they are
sewed together.   There are other machines in use
that page the leaves after the volume is bound, the
principal objection to which appears to be the liability to soil or otherwise injure the binding; notwithstanding this there are some binders who give
them the preference.   Those who have used the
machines of Mr. Griffin speak of them in the highest terms.

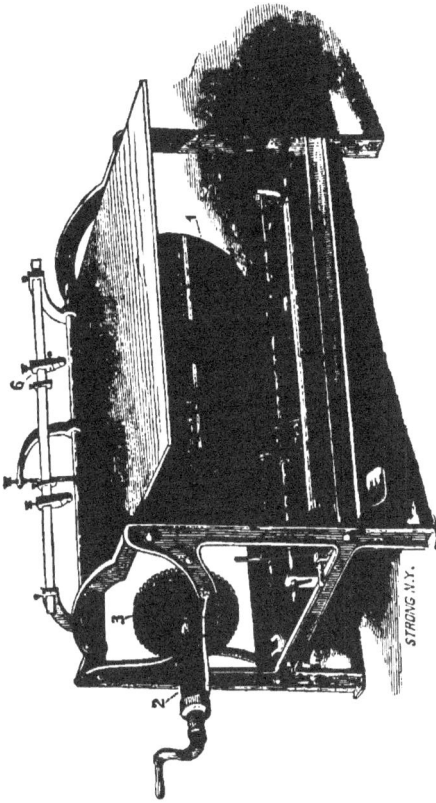

INKS.

To give to the work the best effect, it will be necessary to be provided with good inks, and, it being connected with the subject, some receipts for their preparation are subjoined.

RED INK.

Mix together a quarter of a pound of Brazil dust, a quarter of an ounce of cochineal, a small piece of lump-sugar, and two quarts of vinegar: let these steep ten hours, and afterwards boil them on a slow fire till of a good red colour. When settled, strain the ink through a piece of fine cotton, and bottle it for use.

ANOTHER.

Boil in a quart of soft water a quarter of a pound of Brazil dust; when boiled, put in one ounce of ground alum, one ounce of white stone crystal, and boil for three minutes, and strain.

BLUE INK.

A good blue ink may be obtained by diffusing Prussian blue or indigo through strong gum-water. The common water-colour cakes, diffused also in gum-water, will produce a tolerably good blue for common purposes; but Dyer's blue, diluted with water is preferable to either.

BLACK.

Half a pound of nutgalls, a quarter of a pound of sulphate of zinc. (white vitriol,) two ounces of gum-arabic, and a handful of salt. Boil the nutgalls half an hour in three quarts of soft water, then put the whole together, and let stand for use.

ANOTHER.

For making a larger quantity, put in ten gallons of rain-water, five pounds and a quarter of nutgalls, well bruised, one pound and a half of logwood chips, the like quantity of copperas, and a quarter of a pound of alum. Let them stand a few days, and then add two ounces of gum-arabic and an ounce and a half of verdigris. Stir them all well together two or three times a day for a fortnight or three weeks, and the ink will then be fit for use.

FOLDING.

The whole being ruled, it will be proper to fold the book to the size required into sections for sewing. The number of leaves in each must depend on the thickness of the paper and size of the book, taking care that there are not so many as, when cut, to cause the leaves to start, or so few that the backs will be swollen too much by the thread. Then place the whole evenly in the standing-press for some time, and prepare the end-papers, which must be of blank paper, and outsides, unless the work is

14

of a superior description. Should leather or cloth joints be placed, it will be necessary to sew them on with the end-papers, as before directed.

SEWING.

The sewing of stationery differs much from that of printed books. To allow of the greatest possible strength, elasticity, and freedom, they are sewn on slips of vellum without being marked with the saw, and the whole length of each sheet, with waxed thread. For small books, two slips will be sufficient; for foolscap folio, three will be required; and, where larger, the number must be increased, according to the length of the back, leaving a space of about two inches between each. The plan laid down by *M. Lesne*, (page 27,) might, perhaps, be adopted here with fine and light work to great advantage. The slips should be cut about an inch wide, and of sufficient length to extend about an inch over each side of the back. This portion being bent down at one end of the slips, they must be placed under the end-paper on the table at such places as may be deemed proper, and the section sewn the whole length; and so followed by every portion till the whole are attached in the same man ner, taking care that the slips retain a perpen·

dicular position and that the back be not too much
swollen. Should a morocco joint have been inserted, it must be sewn on with strong silk of the
same colour. When finished, the coloured end-
papers, if any, must be pasted in, and the first and
last ruled leaves similarly attached to the end-
papers. If joints, the same precautions must be
adopted as before directed. The book may then be
beat even on the back and head, placed again in
the laying-press, and glued up, working the brush
well on the back, so as to force the glue between
the sections.

CUTTING.

When the ends and back are dry, this will be the
next operation. Here the fore-edge must be cut
first. It is done before altering the form of the
book, paying great attention to the knife running
evenly across, so that the column nearest the front
is not cut too close, and is parallel to the edge.
When taken out, the back must be rounded with
the hammer, in a greater degree than for other
bindings, and placed again evenly in the standing-
press. After remaining a short time the head and
tail must in like manner be cut, but offer no difference in operation. The book will now be ready for
colouring the edges, the processes of which have

been already described. In England, the large
Dutch marble is generally used for stationers' work.

BOARDING.

The next operation will be the preparation of the
boards for the side-covers, which should be formed
of two or three thin milled boards pasted together.
These must be cut to the proper size with the
plough, so as to leave a perfectly even edge, and
will require to have a larger square allowed for
than is usual in printed books. When cut they must
be pasted together, leaving, if the book is heavy
and the slips on which it is sewn thick, a space at
the back to place them in. The book must now be
head-banded, and then it will be proper to strengthen
the back of the book by glueing across, on the
spaces between the slips, strong pieces of canvas,
and at the head and tail a piece of calf, leaving
projections on each side to be attached to the board.
For additional firmness, it was formerly usual,
where the work was of a superior description, to
sew the length of the book with catgut in about ten
or fourteen places, according to the thickness. This
is done by placing three strips of strong leather in
spaces between the vellum ones, and sewing as at
first, by which means the gut, crossing over the

leather and under the vellum slips on the back, appears inside on the spaces where no thread has before passed. For ornament, another thread is twisted round the gut on the back, so as to present the appearance of a double cord. These matters being adjusted, the slips of calf at the head and tail must be let in by cutting the end of the waste leaf and placing them under. The other slips, of every description, after trimming, must then be put into the space left between the boards, which should be previously well pasted or glued, the boards placed nearly half an inch from the back, and perfectly square on the sides, and the whole screwed tightly in the standing-press for some time.

THE SPRING-BACK.

There are numerous ways of forming this description of back, and as generally adopted in different offices. As in other particulars, two or three of the best will here be given: 1. Having ascertained the width and length of the back, and provided a piece of strong pasteboard, or thin milled board, of little more than twice the width, fold one side rather more than half, and then the other, so that the middle space left will be the exact size required, which should be about a quarter of an inch

wider than the back of the book; then cut evenly
another piece, a little less than the width, then
another still less, and so on for six or seven, lessen-
ing the width each time till the last is merely a
narrow slip. Let the edges of the first, or cover
for the whole, be pared, and laid open on the table;
then glue the middle space, and place thereon the
largest slip, which also glue, and add the next in
size, proceeding in like manner till the smallest is
fixed, taking especial care that each occupies the
exact centre of the one on which it is placed.
Finally, glue the whole space and the two side-slips
of the first, which must be brought over and firmly
rubbed down. Shape it to the curve of the back
of the book, either on the back or a wooden roller
of the same size, and leave it to dry, when the head
and tail must be cut to the proper length with the
shears. For greater security the whole is often
covered with linen cloth.

2. Cut a piece of firm milled board to the size
required, and pare down the edges; then hold the
board to the fire till it is found soft enough to model
almost into any shape, and form to the back as
above directed. The board is sometimes wetted,
but does not answer so well.

3. A beaten iron plate of the exact size, and covered with parchment or leather.

Numerous patents have been obtained for this description of back, but none have been found to answer the purpose, on account of the metal cutting through the parchment or leather.

The spring-back is only used for the superior kind of account-books; for common work, a piece of thin pasteboard is merely laid on the back before covering, the stress on the back being small.

To prevent the manufactured back slipping during the operation of covering, it is laid on, and a piece of cloth glued over and attached to the sides, similarly to the back of a half-bound book. This tends also to materially strengthen the back.

COVERING.

The materials generally used for stationery-binding are russia, rough calf, green and white vellum, and rough sheep, according to the value of the work. Previous to pasting on vellum, the book should be covered with a piece of strong paper, as if for boards. The process is the same as for other bindings; but when completed, it will be necessary to put the book in the standing-press, having pieces of cane or wood for the purpose placed between the

boards and the back, so as to form a bold groove,
and force the leather close on the edge of the spring-
back.   Previous to and after pressing, the headbands must be squarely set, taking care to rub out
any wrinkles that may have been formed in turning
in the cover.   Should the book be very large, it
may be advisable to give it a nip in the press immediately after folding in the fore-edges of the
boards, and then finish the covering by turning in
the head and tail.

As circumstances — such as the fancy of some
previous workman, or coloured vellum not to be
obtained so early as required — may make it necessary to execute the proper colours, the proceedings are here given.

GREEN.

Put one ounce of verdigris and one ounce of
white wine vinegar into a bottle, and place them
near the fire for five days, shaking it three or four
times each day.   Wash the vellum over with weak
pearlash, and then colour it to the shade desired.

RED.

To one pint of white wine vinegar, put a quarter
of a pound of Brazil dust and a piece of alum.

Cork the mixture up ; let it stand in a warm place for two or three days.

PURPLE.

Proceed as for the *red*, substituting logwood chips for the Brazil dust.

YELLOW.

Half an ounce of turmeric to half a pint of spirits of wine, prepared as above.

BLACK.

Wash the vellum over three times with the red, and while wet colour with strong marbling-ink.

Marbles and other designs may be formed on white vellum ; but, as the proceedings have been so fully entered into before, it will not be necessary here to repeat them. Where russia bands are not added, the end-papers must now be pasted down, and the lettering, &c. proceeded with. If bands are attached, the pasting down of the end-papers and joints must be deferred till they are executed.

RUSSIA BANDS.

To give to large books the greatest possible degree of strength, it is usual to affix Russia bands to them. They are called *single* when they extend

about half-way down the sides, and *double* when
those at the head and tail reach to the corners of
the boards, and are turned over the edges in the
same manner as the cover. For *single;*—having
ascertained the breadth by dividing the back with
the compasses into *seven* spaces, cut three pieces
of russia perfectly square and the exact size of the
spaces they are to occupy, and paste them on the
second, fourth, and *sixth* divisions of the back,
thereby leaving in sight the first, third, fifth, and
seventh spaces with the cover only; draw them
squarely on the sides, and place the volume in the
press, with the rods fixed to force the russia into
the joints, as before directed, and then leave to dry.
When *double* bands are to be placed on a book,
divide the back into five spaces, or seven if four
bands. The middle band or bands will be short,
like those above, and placed on in the same manner; but those at the head and tail, which extend
their whole length, to the fore-edge of the boards,
will require paring on the edge intended to be
turned in at the headbands and over the boards of
the book, cutting the corners and squaring the edges
as in covering. When done, press the whole with
rods as before, to cause the russia to adhere well
and evenly to the vellum or calf, and leave it to dry.

CLASPS, CORNERS, AND BRASS BANDS.

Clasps are sometimes affixed to the better kind of stationery books, as keeping them closed when not in use tends much towards their preservation. And for still greater security, they are often further protected with brass corners or bands. To hide the projection the clasps would make on the fore-edge, that part of the board must be cut away to admit the clasp, so that when fixed it will be even with the edge of the board. For the corners and bands this is not done; but, to insure a finished appearance in the whole, the workman's attention must be directed to their fitting exactly in every particular of length, breadth, and thickness. The clasps may be purchased of the makers, but it may be found necessary to place the making of the bands and corners in the hands of the brass-worker, to whom particular directions and sizes must be given. They must fit tightly to the boards, run exactly parallel with the edges, and have the holes for the rivets drilled through previous to placing on. Where corners are put on, no bands will be required. Bands which extend from the back to the fore-edge and form a corner equal to the breadth of the band, being squarely soldered in front, are placed at the head and tail of the book, and fastened with rivets in the following manner, as are also the clasps and corners:—Pierce the boards with a fine bodkin in such places as are previously drilled in the brass, and force through brass rivets of a length sufficient to project about the eighth of an inch, and with heads made to fit exactly to the cavities formed in the bands; then fasten them firmly, by placing the heads of each on an iron and beating down with a hammer the part projecting inside, till it is smooth and even with the surface. Bosses, which are seen fixed on the middle of the boards of old books, particularly of early-bound Bibles, &c., in churches, are fastened in the same manner.

FINISHING.

The placing of lettering-pieces, gilding, and blind-tooling, is exactly the same as for printed books. Rough calf must be dressed with pumice-stone, cleaned with a brush, and ornamented blind, with the tools very hot, to form a dark impression. Vellum will require the tools cooler than calf. The book now being ready for the use of the accountant necessarily closes the details of this description of binding.

BOARDING.

In large places, this is another distinct branch of the art, and consists of simply covering the book with coloured paper or other common substance. In small towns, it must necessarily be executed jointly with the other branches; but so ample and minute has been the detail of the various manipulations in a previous part of this work, that, in attempting a description of BOARDING, little can be said without repetition. This style, too, being the commonest mode of doing up books in this country, also places the subject, under any circumstances, in a position requiring but little remark. Previous, therefore, to speaking of the few processes that are peculiar to boarding, it will only be necessary to observe that the folding, pressing, sewing, backing, boarding, covering, and pasting down, are the same as for regularly-bound books. It remains, then, to add that the books will not require beating, and, for common boards, are never cut round the edges. The leaves are only dressed with the trimming-knife previous to rounding the back, so as to present as neat an appearance as possible, by removing every portion of the paper projecting over the general line. For greater strength to the back, a piece

15

of paper must be pasted in the centre of the coloured
paper previously to applying it on the volume.
When covered and pasted down, the printed label
must be fixed evenly on the back, and the book
will be finished.

CLOTH-WORK.

In the year 1825 a great revolution in boarding
was begun by the introduction of cloth covers in
place of the drab-coloured paper previously in use.
The late Archibald Leighton, of London, was the inventor; and Mr. Pickering was the first publisher who
adopted it. The first cloth covers had printed labels;
but very soon Mr. Leighton made the discovery that
cloth could be stamped with gold very beautifully.
Lord Byron's works (the edition in 17 volumes)
were the first books to which gold-lettering on cloth
was applied. Cloth-work is now done with full gilt
sides and back and gilt edges; but, from the tem-
porary character of this style, the question may
arise whether it is not a useless expenditure of time
and money to produce it. But, so long as the
public remain unacquainted with its want of capability for use, and desire a mass of gold upon the
sides,—so long, in fact, as there is a large class
who desire books for mere show and not for use,—

it will be the interest of publishers to gratify them by furnishing cloth-gilt work.

Expedition being so important in cloth-work, a machine has been introduced to facilitate the operation of sawing the backs, and it is now in general use for the purpose. The appended cut gives an accurate idea of the machine as manufactured by W. O. Hickok, Harrisburg, Pa.

For this and all other species of case-work (morocco is sometimes done in this manner) the lining-
papers are inserted and pasted over so as to adhere
to the end-paper, and the slips, having been cut
short, are scraped or rubbed smooth. The volumes
are then knocked up and touched on the back in
one or two places with the glue-brush. They
are then cut upon the fore-edge, by being placed
between two boards, one of which is precisely
the width that it is intended to cut the volumes ;
the boards and books are placed upon the laying-
press, and the backs knocked evenly up ; the whole
is then placed in the laying-press, and cut with the
plough. The back-board being wider than the
front, the knife cuts against it. If the volumes are
small, a number may be cut at the same time. This
mode of cutting is called " steamboating." After
the whole lot that the workman "has on" have been
cut on the fronts, they are then placed between
cutting-boards again, of the proper size, and
knocked up on the head; they are then laid upon
the press, with the runner or front-board up ; the
board is then moved about a quarter of an inch
below the heads of the volumes as they are arranged
in layers or piles. The workman will then grasp
the boards firmly, so as not to allow the books to

slip, and place them in the cutting-press, and, after screwing it up tightly with the press-pin, proceed to cut the heads in the same manner as the fronts. After this is done, unscrew the press partially, so as to allow the volumes to be turned without slipping in the tub; then, with one hand beneath the press, depress one end of the boards, while the other is elevated, until the whole is turned completely over, with the tails upward. The runner is adjusted even with the check of the press, the press is screwed up, and the volumes cut at the tail. If the edges are to be gilt, they are now prepared for that operation. Afterwards they are glued upon the backs and rounded, care being taken not to start the sheets or mark the gilding upon the fore-edge with the thumb. They are then backed in the same manner as bound books, except that they have larger joints. Care is requisite at the ends, or the blows of the hammer will crush the paper and thus give the gilding an unsightly ap-pearance at the joints.

A machine has been invented for the purpose of backing books, and it appears to be growing in favour for cloth-work, and, in fact, for all work where expedition is a primary essential. It is the invention of Mr. Sanborn, of Portland, Maine.
15*

The annexed cut gives an idea of the general appearance of the machine.

The next process is lining the backs, which is done by pasting strips of paper or muslin upon the back, having it of sufficient width to cover the joints on each side. The volumes are then prepared for the cases, which have been previously got ready. The boards are cut to a uniform square size by the table-shears. The cloth covers, after having been cut out, have the corners cut off to a pattern made for the purpose, just sufficient to allow them to lap when the cloth is turned over the edge of the boards. The cover is then glued

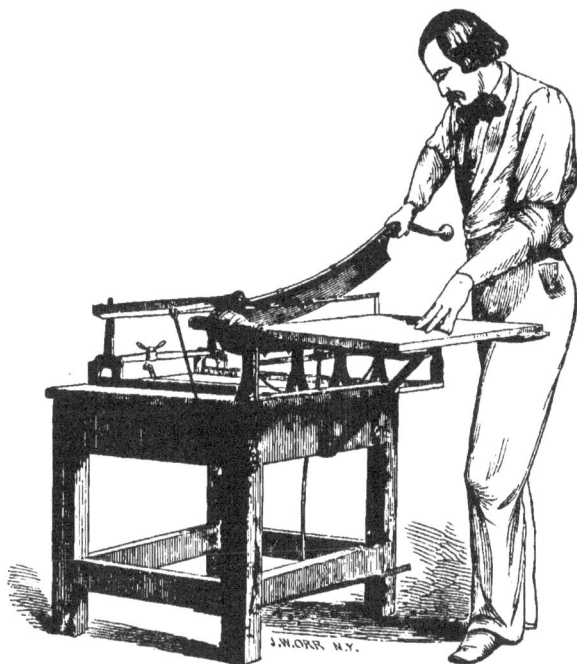

TABLE-SHEARS.

equally over, and the ⊤ square laid upon it,—the
square having been made of the proper width to
allow for the back, joints, and groove of the volume.
A board is then laid on each side of the centre of
the square; the latter is then lifted off, and a strip
of paper, of the length of the boards and nearly
the width of the back of the book, placed between

the boards. The cloth projecting beyond the boards is then turned over their edges. The cover is then turned over, and the cloth rubbed smooth on the sides by means of a woollen or cotton pad. It is then placed between pasteboards to dry. After the cases are all made and have become perfectly dry, they are ready for stamping. Cloth for ordinary stamping requires no preparation, but if the stamp be large or very heavy it will be safer to use a coat of size. For this purpose Russian isinglass is preferable; fresh glaire will answer the same purpose. After the cases are stamped, the volumes being ready, they are arranged with their heads the same way, and the end-paper of the volume is pasted equally over. The book is then laid, pasted side downwards, upon a case, adjusting the squares properly at the same time; the other end-paper is then pasted, and the other board or side of the case drawn over the back and placed upon the volume. After a number are pasted, they are placed in pressing-boards having a brass band affixed to the edges of the boards. The band, being rather wider than the thickness of the board, causes a slight projection. The volumes are adjusted in the pressing-boards in such a manner as to cause the back and joint of the volumes to be on the outer, while the pasteboard is on the inner, side of the brass rim. In this position the volumes are placed in the standing-press and screwed tightly down; they are then tapped lightly at the heads with a small backing-hammer, and allowed to remain until dry. They are then taken out, and the end-papers opened up or separated with a folding-stick. They are then ready for the bookseller's shelves.

PART III.

ORNAMENTAL ART.

IN treating upon this subject, we are led back
to the land of the Pharaohs; for the earliest Art
records that have come down to us (and, perhaps,
the most perfect) are from the banks of the Nile,
remarkable for their severely massive character,
calm and frigid. The few ornamental details are
chosen rather for their symbolical than æsthetic
beauty, consisting of local forms slightly conven-
tionalized and heightened with colour. Their ornaments were types and symbols intended to address
themselves to the eye, heart, and soul of the be-
holder, the most frequent in recurrence being the
winged globe,—a sacred emblem the Egyptians used
in their ornamental designs,—the human figure, their
sacred animals, and the lotus, reed, asp, and papyrus. Upon the capitals of Egyptian columns are
represented nearly all the flowers peculiar to the
country, the petals, capsules, pistils, seeds, and

most minute parts, being often exhibited. Capitals
are often seen resembling a vase, and at other times
a bell reversed. There is little in this style applicable to the decoration of books, unless it be upon
works relating to Egypt. Then its symbols afford
the binder an opportunity to employ its symbolic
ornamentation.

ASSYRIAN AND ANCIENT PERSIAN.

Of this style it is only lately that we have become
slightly acquainted; and, though partly coeval with
the Egyptian, the Assyrians have borrowed little
from them, the details being remarkable for their
classic character, at times approaching the Ionic,
but greatly dependent upon animal forms for its
ornamentation, and upon painting and sculpture for
its expression. The forms, often graceful, are less
arbitrary than the Egyptian, (where symbolism is
paramount,) containing those elements afterwards
elaborated into beauty by the Greeks. There is an
appropriate fitness in Assyrian ornament that con-
stitutes one of its prominent characteristics. In addition to animals, the pomegranate, fir-cones, lotus-
flower and reeds, rosettes, and a fan-shaped
ornament supposed to be the origin of the Greek
honeysuckle, distinguish the Assyrian style.

GREEK.

Under the ancient Greeks, Art attained a refined and exalted character, material beauty being developed to the utmost; elegance of proportion, chaste simplicity, and conventionalism, triumphant; symbolism disregarded. The principal elements of Greek ornament were the honeysuckle, the lotus-leaves, the wave-line and scroll, the zig-zag, and the universal fret. The beauty of Grecian ornament consists in its equality of foliage, starting-points, stalks, and groundwork. Its running figures are well adapted to and are employed for rolls, in side-finishing, and the proportions of this style of Art should be carefully studied by the finisher.

ETRUSCAN.

Simplicity and elegance of form, combined with strong contrast in colour, constitute the distinguishing marks of this style. The Etruscan vases still form models for the artist. The novel appearance of these vessels, all uniformly painted with a tracery of black on a natural groundwork of brownish red, is extremely pleasing, proving the high artistic capability of their makers. In the British Museum there is one room entirely devoted to a collection of these remains of ancient Art. This style is ap-

proached in its effects by inlaying with black upon
a brownish red. A copy of Caxton's " Recuyell of
the Historyes of Troye," bound in this style by Whit-
taker, has been highly extolled. It is in the possession of the Marquis of Bath. The general effects
of this style are represented by a style now much
in vogue, called antique, a reddish-brown morocco
being stamped upon so as to produce a dark or
black figure thereon ; but the character of the ornaments are generally dissimilar.

ROMAN.

Roman art is a redundant elaboration of the
Greek, in which purity gives way to richness,
grotesque combinations become common, and false
principles creep in. Mosaic pavements are rendered
pictorial by the introduction of light and shade, the
flat and round not kept distinct. In the remains
of Pompeii we find the degradation of classic Art by
the violation of true principles. There is nothing
in this style to commend it to the artist, especially
in decorating books.

BYZANTINE, LOMBARD, NORMAN.

These varieties of kindred ornament, commencing
with the rise of Christianity, were founded on classic
16

details, having a distinct expression of their own. There is much symbolism in the Byzantine, but all are appropriate to their several wants,—the parts rich, judiciously disposed, and purely conventional. In these styles, so intimately connected, we find the interlaced strap-work that suggested Gothic tracery to the great mediæval artists.

MOORISH.

The decorative art of the Arabs is more conventional than any other, it being in most cases extremely difficult to trace the origin of their forms. All animal representations are strictly excluded by the religion of Mohammed. The union of geometrical with floral forms seems to have supplied the expression, many ornaments resembling the ovary of plants, transversely cut and connected with crystalline shapes. The abstract and superficial treatment is perfect, the forms are extremely graceful, and the colouring gorgeous. The interlaced strapwork is highly elaborated. This style is sometimes called the Arabesque, and forms the chief decoration of the Alhambra, an ancient fortress and residence of the Moorish monarchs of Granada. For grace and liveliness this style is unrivalled, and it affords many useful and beautiful hints to the finisher in his hand-tooling, and is well calculated to produce fine effects in stamps designed for the embossing-press.

GOTHIC.

The Gothic is founded upon geometrical forms. The strap-work of former styles is elaborated into tracery, the main lines being circular or curved, starting from vertical lines, ending in points, enclosing spaces divided and subdivided in the same manner, further decorated with conventional ornaments derived from local nature. For bookbinding it is sometimes employed, but without much judgment. The judicious finisher will reject it on account of its inapplicability to superficial decoration.

THE RENAISSANCE.

The Renaissance or Revival arose in Italy in the fifteenth century, by the appropriation of classic details in connection with prior styles, the traditionary giving way to selection and freedom; Art gaining but few entirely new forms, rather subjecting all that had gone before to a new treatment, which in the hands of the great artists of the period produced agreeable results, showing the importance of general design, rendering even incongruous materials pleasing from that cause alone

The Cinque-cento has been considered the goal of the Renaissance and its characteristics,—strap, tracery, arabesque, and pierced scroll-work, a mixture of the conventional with natural forms, and every detail of ancient Art,—producing, under different masters, varied results. Thus, in Raphael's Loggie of the Vatican are to be found, as at Pompeii, elements piled one above the other, without any regard to construction. The same with the works of Julio Romano at Mantua,—painted imitation of bas-reliefs suspended above fountains, temples, &c., the parts often finely drawn and treated, but, taken as a whole, little removed from the absurd, quite unlike the works of the Greeks and Etruscans they sought to rival.

ELIZABETHAN.

The Elizabethan was an English version of the Renaissance, being a special elaboration of the strap and bolt-work, and has been highly useful to the stamp-cutter. Many of its forms can be advantageously employed by the finisher.

LOUIS QUATORZE.

This distinct expression of Art is of Italian origin, being the last of the Renaissance, and end of ornamental styles. It consists of scrolls and shells, an alternation of curves and hollows, the concave and convex in contrast, the broken surfaces affording a brilliant play of light and shade. The effect when gilt being extremely magnificent, colour was abandoned, construction hidden, and symmetry often disregarded, especially in its decline. As to superficial treatment, flat surfaces were studiously avoided, and the few that remained were treated pictorially, in a mellifluous, pastoral style, known as that of Watteau. Under Louis XV. the forms degenerated: symmetrical balance and flow of line were disregarded, giving way to the degraded ornamentation called the Rococo—the prevailing style of the last and earlier part of the present century—depriving Europe for more than one hundred years of true superficial decoration, without which no Art can be considered complete. An attempt at this style may be seen upon the sides of some of the gaudily-gilt albums and books of like character. No finisher need cultivate a love for it, for it is the aversion of all refined artists.

FINISHING.

TASTE AND DESIGN.

It is of the utmost importance to a young workman that he have correct ideas in regard to taste, and be able to distinguish it from caprice or mere fancy. It is in the power of all to acquire a correct taste, for it is governed by laws that can be easily learned, and they are unchangeable. Taste may be said to be a perception and an appreciation of the principles of beauty and harmony as revealed by Nature through Art. Nothing contrary to nature, no violation of any law of proportion or of fitness, can be in good taste. The amateur and book-collector, in commencing the foundation of a library, will do well to pause before they adopt a species of binding that will in after years create a feeling of annoyance, and perhaps lead to pecuniary sacrifice.

A recent writer upon the New York Exhibition of the Industry of all Nations discourses thus :— "We call bookbinding an art; and when we consider all that is necessary to the perfect covering of a fine book, it must be admitted to be an art; less important, it is true, but similar in kind to architecture.

"The first requisition upon the skill of the binder is to put the book into a cover which will effectually protect it, and at the same time permit it to be used with ease. If he do not accomplish this, his most elaborate exhibition of ornamental skill is worth nothing; for he fails in the very end for which his services are required. It was in this regard, too, that most of our binders failed in past years. Who that remembers the hideous, harsh, speckled sheep covers which deformed our booksellers' shelves not long ago, can forget the added torment which they inflicted upon their unhappy purchaser, by curling up palpably before his very eyes, as he passed his first evening over them, and by casting out loose leaves or whole signatures before he had finished his first perusal? In those days, too, there was morocco binding, with a California of gold upon the sides; and such morocco! it felt to the fingers like a flattened nutmeg-grater, seeming to protect the book by making it painful for any one to touch it. This was as useless as the humbler though not more vulgar sheep. It would hardly last through the holiday season on the centre-table which it was made to adorn.

"The binder's next task is to give his work the substantial appearance without which the eye of

the connoisseur will remain unsatisfied. The volume must not only be well protected, but seem so.
It should be solid, compact, square-edged, and en-
closed in firm boards of a stoutness proportionate
to its size, and these should be covered with leather
at once pliable and strong. Unless it present this
appearance, it will be unsatisfactory in spite of the
richest colours and the most elaborate ornament.
Thus far the mere mechanical skill of the binder
goes. In the choice of his style of binding, and
in the decoration of his book, if he perform his task
with taste and skill, he rises to the rank of an
artist.

" The fitness of the binding to the character of
the volume which it protects, though little regarded
by many binders, and still less by those for whom
they work, is of the first importance. Suppose
Moore's Lalla Rookh bound in rough sheep, with
dark russia back and corners, like a merchant's
ledger, or Johnson's folio Dictionary in straw-
coloured morocco elaborately gilded, and lined with
pale blue watered-silk, is there an eye, no matter
how uneducated, which would not be shocked at the
incongruity? Each book might be perfectly protected, open freely, and exhibit evidence of great
mechanical and artistic skill on the part of the

binder; but his atrocious taste would insure him a just and universal condemnation. And yet there are violations of fitness to be seen daily, on the majority of public and private shelves, little less outrageous than those we have supposed. Books of poetry, and illustrated works on art bound in sober speckled or tree-marbled calf, with little gold upon the backs and sides, and none upon the edges! Histories, statistical works, and books of reference, in rich morocco, splendidly gilded!—the idea that the styles ought to change places seeming never to enter the heads of the possessors of these absurdly-covered volumes. But a little reflection by any person of taste, and power to discern the eternal fitness of things, will make it apparent that there should be congruity and adaptation in the binding of books. Sober, practical volumes should be correspondingly covered; calf and russia leather, with marbled paper and edges, become them; while works of imagination, such as poetry and books of engravings, demand rich morocco, fanciful ornaments, and gilding. To bind histories, philosophical works, dictionaries, books of reference and the like, in plain calf or dark russia,—travels, novels, essays, and the lighter kind of prose writing, in tinted calf or pale russia with gilding,—poetry in

full morocco richly gilded, and works on art in half
morocco, with the top edge only cut and gilded,—
seems a judicious partition of the principal styles
of binding. The margins of an illustrated work
on Art should never be cut away, except where it is
absolutely necessary for the preservation of the
book from dust, and the convenience of turning the
leaves—that is, at the top. It is well here to enter
a protest against the indiscriminate use of the antique style of binding, with dark-brown calf, bevelled
boards, and red edges. This is very well in its
place; but it should be confined to prose works of
authors who wrote not later than one hundred and
fifty years ago. What propriety is there in putting
Scott, or Irving, or Dickens, or Longfellow, in such
a dress?"

Hartley Coleridge's opinion on the subject of
taste in Bookbinding is thus given :—" The binding
of a book should always suit its complexion. Pages
venerably yellow should not be cased in military
morocco, but in sober brown russia. Glossy hotpressed paper looks best in vellum. We have sometimes seen a collection of whitey-brown black-letter
ballads, &c. so gorgeously tricked out that they
remind us of the pious liberality of the Catholics,
who dress in silk and gold the images of saints,

part of whose saintship consisted in wearing rags and hair-cloth. The costume of a volume should also be in keeping with its subject, and with the character of its author. How absurd to see the works of William Penn in flaming scarlet, and George Fox's Journal in bishops' purple! Theology should be solemnly gorgeous. History should be ornamented after the antique and Gothic fashion; works of science, as plain as is consistent with dignity; poetry, *simplex munditis.*"

And it may not be irrelevant here to introduce the opinion of Dr. Dibdin, whose connection with some of the first libraries in England, and whose intimate knowledge of all the great book-collectors of the same, must tend to stamp him as a good authority on the subject:—

"The general appearance of one's library is by no means a matter of mere foppery or indifference; it is a sort of cardinal point, to which the tasteful collector does well to attend. You have a right to consider books, as to their *outsides,* with the eye of a *painter;* because this does not militate against the proper use of the contents.

"Be sparing of red morocco or vellum. They have each so distinct, or what painters call spotty, an appearance, that they should be introduced but cir-

cumspectly. Morocco, I frankly own, is my favourite surtout; and the varieties of them—*blue,*
(dark and light,) *orange, green,* and *olive-colour*—
are especially deserving of your attention.

The colour of the binding may often be in harmony with its contents. Books of poetry may be
red, or light green, or blue, and have as much
ornament as may be desired. And Fine Art books,
above all others, ought to rejoice in beautiful
coloured moroccos and gorgeous ornaments. In the
British Museum, books of divinity are bound in
blue, history in red, poetry in yellow, and biography
in olive.

" Let *russia* claim your volumes of architecture
or other antiquities, of topography, of lexicography,
and of other works of reference. Let your romances
and chronicles aspire to *morocco* or *velvet;* though,
upon second thoughts, *russia* is well suited to history and chronicles. And for your fifteeners, or
volumes printed in the fifteenth century, whether
Greek, Latin, Italian, or English, let me entreat you
invariably to use *morocco:* for theology, *dark blue,*
black, or *damson-colour;* for history, *red* or *dark*
green; while, in large paper quartos, do not fail to
remember the *peau de veau* (calf) of the French,
with gilt upon marbled edges. My abhorrence of

hogskin urges me to call upon you to swear eternal enmity to that engenderer of mildew and mischief. Indeed, at any rate, it is a clumsy coat of mail. For your Italian and French, especially in long suites, bespeak what is called *French calf binding*, spotted, variegated, or marbled on the sides, well covered with ornament on the back, and, when the work is worthy of it, with gilt on the edges. Let your English octavos of history or belles-lettres breathe a quiet tone of chastely-gilded white calf with marbled edges; while the works of our better-most poets should be occasionally clothed in a morocco exterior."

The further opinion of the doctor on the style of ornament, &c. in gilding, will be given in its proper place, and which, with that cited above, may be safely acted upon by the binder, blended with such additions as his own taste may dictate.

It is in this state that the defects of forwarding will become more apparent, and which no tact or ingenuity of the finisher can effectually remedy; for, unless the bands are square, the joints free, and the whole book geometrically just, the defect, whatever it may be, will appear throughout, and tend to destroy the beauty of every subsequent operation,

17

from the constraint required to make the general appearance of the work effective.

Before proceeding to a description of the various manipulations required in gilding a book, it will be necessary to direct the attention of the young workman again to what has been advanced relative to care and attention in previous parts of this work, and follow up the remarks there made with others on the taste necessary to be displayed in this most important part of the art of bookbinding. When it is considered that the most celebrated artists have arrived at the eminence awarded to them not only through the elasticity, solidity, and squareness of their bindings, but also from the judicious choice of their ornaments for gilding, and the precision and beauty with which they have been executed, it cannot be too strongly impressed on the workman that this should ever occupy his first attention. Nothing is so disagreeable to the eye as injudicious or badly-executed ornaments; while with chaste and classical embellishments, tastefully applied, an appearance of richness is produced on the volumes that cannot fail to give satisfaction to the most fastidious critic. The sides of the volumes present the field most favourable for the display of ornamental taste, admitting, from their extent, the execution of the

most complicated designs. This elaborate style of
ornament has been carried to such perfection and
splendour as, in many instances, to have occupied
several days in the execution of one side alone; but
it is only by the most vigorous application, greatest
care, and correct taste, that proficiency therein can
be attained. With these, success will soon crown the
endeavours of the workman; and he will have the
satisfaction of finding himself able to imitate any
pattern, however difficult, as well as to execute many
new designs and compartments, of which, till he
applied himself, he had not previously an idea.

As regards the style of ornament, it must be left
to taste; but, as before promised, it will now be
proper to introduce the remarks of Dr. Dibdin on
the general effect of gilding and blind tooling,
leaving the detail to be suggested to the mind of
the gilder.

" First, let your books be well and evenly lettered,
and let a tolerable portion of ornament be seen upon
the backs of them. I love what is called an *overcharged back.* At first the appearance may be
flaunting and garish; but time, which mellows down
book ornaments as well as human countenances,
will quickly obviate this inconvenience; and about
a twelvemonth, or six months added to the said

twelvemonth, will work miracles upon the appearance of your book. Do not be meagre of your ornaments on the back, and never suffer *blind tooling* wholly to pervade a folio or quarto; for, by so doing, you convert what should look like a *book* into a piece of mahogany furniture.

"In large libraries there should not be too much blind tooling or too great a want of gilt. No doubt the ornament should be as appropriate as possible to the book. One could not endure gingerbread-gilt *Bibles* and *Prayer-Books*, or *Chronicles* or *Dictionaries*, or other books of reference. Let these have a subdued decoration on their backs; bands only full-gilt, or a running edge-tool in the centres of them, with small ornaments between the bands.

"I would recommend the lettering of a volume to be as *full* as possible; yet sententiousness must sometimes be adopted. The lines should be straight, and the letters of one and the same form or character within the line; yet the name of the author may be executed a size larger than that of the date or place of its execution, and the lettering may be between the top and bottom bands, or it may occupy the spaces between three bands, or even more. Re-letter old books perpendicularly, as was the custom. In all fresh bindings, however, prefer horizontal to perpendicular lettering."*

It remains to urge that particular attention be paid to the lettering of books being their right titles, as the contrary will present to the judicious an effect the most disagreeable, and may be the cause of producing dissatisfaction with the whole of the binding in the mind of the owner; and also to avoid the contrast which the different shade or colour of new lettering-pieces will give to some bindings.

As it is requisite that the workman should form an idea of the style and design to be executed on the volume before he prepares it for gilding, we will proceed to point out the peculiarities of some of the most prominent styles and of the tools required to produce them. We hope to convey a faithful idea of the latter with the aid of the tools and ornaments executed expressly for this work by Gaskill, Copper & Fry, bookbinders' tool-

---

* We sometimes fear that Dr. Dibden's commendation of an overcharged back has produced a bad effect. It should be borne in mind that, when the doctor wrote, calf was the prevailing material employed in binding, and that of a light colour.

17*

cutters, Philadelphia, who have secured for themselves, by their taste and skill, an enviable reputation as artists.   Plate I. contains an illustration of
the species of ornament termed

THE ALDINE STYLE,

Which derives its name from a noted printer named
Aldus Manutius, a Roman by birth, who was born
in the year 1446 or 1447.   His Christian name,
Aldus, was a contraction of Theobaldus ; and to
this surname he sometimes added the appellation of
Pius, or Bassianus, or Romanus.   The first of these
appellatives was assumed by Aldus from his having
been the tutor of Albertus Pius, a prince of the
noble house of Carpi ; and the second was derived
from the birthplace of the printer—namely, Bassian,
a small town in the Duchy of Lermonetta.

Aldus is supposed to have taken up his residence
at Venice, as the favourite city wherein to mature
his plans, about the year 1488 ; and about 1494–95
he there put forth the first production of his press.
He introduced Roman types of a neater cut than
had previously been in use, and invented that
beautiful letter which is now known as *Italic*,
though, in the first instance, it was termed *Venetian*, from Manutius being a resident of Venice

when he brought it to perfection; but, not long after, it was dedicated to the State of Italy, to prevent any dispute that might arise from other nations claiming a priority, as was the case concerning the first inventor of printing.

Prior to the time of Aldus, the only points used in punctuation were the comma, colon, and full-point or period; but he invented the semicolon, gave a better shape to the comma, and connected the punctuation by assigning to the various points more proper places. About the period of his marriage, (in 1500,) he invented a mode of imposing a work in such a manner that two languages might be interleaved and bound together, or separately, at the option of the purchaser; and, about the same date, he printed the first leaf, in folio, of a proposed edition of the BIBLE in the Hebrew, Greek, and Latin languages; so that he has the honour of having first suggested the plan of a Polyglott Bible. However, the plan failed of being then carried into effect. Printing different languages in opposite columns was not accomplished till 1530.

The mind of Aldus was entirely engaged in the care of his printing-house; for, as soon as he had ordered his other necessary affairs, he shut himself up in his study, where he employed himself in

revising his Greek and Latin MSS., reading the
letters which he received from the learned out of all
parts of the world, and writing answers to them.
To prevent interruption by impertinent visits, he
caused the following inscription to be placed over his
door :—" *Whoever you are Aldus earnestly entreats
you to despatch your business as soon as possible,
and then depart: unless you come hither, like another Hercules, to lend him some friendly assistance ; for here will be work sufficient to employ
you and as many as enter this place.*"

The mark or device which Aldus—who died in
1515—made use of to distinguish works issued from
his press was an anchor, round which a dolphin
seemed to twist. It must be familiar to every amateur,—Mr. Pickering, the London publisher, having
adopted the Aldine anchor as his device. To attempt
any description of the Aldine class of tools would
be superfluous after so fair a specimen in the illustration. It will be perceived they are entirely free
from shading, and, consequently, much more effective for that description of work for which they are
generally used,—viz., blind tooling. Both tools and
patterns are much lighter and more ornamental
than the old Monastic school, of which the Aldine
in some degree partook.

Upon the same plate there is exhibited the arrangement of a back-panel and tools in the

MONTAGUE STYLE,

Which derives its name from Montague, (of the firm of Montague and Johnson,) a bookbinder of considerable eminence, who flourished about the year 1780. The chief features of this style are corners and centre, filled up with stops, &c. similar to illustration. The tools are of an open, leafy description, flowing from a stem free from any thing of the scroll or curl. The panel given has been copied from a book supposed to have been done by Montague himself. The bar, or barleycorn, on the head and tail and on the bands, likewise on the insides and edges. Books in volumes, pieced red and green on adjoining panels, frequently a lozenge of red on the second piece, and filled up with corners and stops similar to the other panels; sometimes both pieces green; sides generally plain, or a flowery flowing roll, for which a two-line is now usually substituted; sewed on raised bands; colour, brown calf, sometimes highly sprinkled.

There is also upon Plate I. an illustration of

THE HARLEIAN STYLE,

A style not behind Montague in beauty of ornament, and superior in elegance and variety of arrangement. Before entering into a description of
the style, we will give what information we have
gained respecting its founder, trusting that it will
not be unacceptable. We find that "Robert Harley, Esq., of Frampton-Bryan, in the county of
Hereford, (the gentleman from whom the style
derives its name,) was in 1700 chosen Speaker
of the House of Commons, and in May, 1711, he
was created Earl of Oxford and Mortimer, and five
days afterwards was promoted to the important
station of Lord High-Treasurer of Great Britain."
In the Preface to the Harleian MSS., now in the
British Museum, speaking of Mr. Harley, it states
that "his innate love of books was such as to determine him in early life to undertake the formation of
a new library, regardless of the disadvantages with
which he must contend, as great exertions had previously been made in collecting MSS. for the Bodleian,
Cottonian, and other valuable though smaller collections, so that the prospect of forming a new library
with any considerable number of MSS. was indeed
very unpromising. But, urged on by a love of learning,

and a strong desire to search into the transactions of former ages, determined Mr. Harley to purchase whatever curious MSS. he could meet with, more especially such as might in any wise tend to explain and illustrate the history, laws, customs, and antiquities, of his native country. The principal point which the founder of the Harleian Library had in view was the establishment of a MS. English Historical Library, and the rescuing from oblivion and destruction of such valuable records of our national antiquities as had escaped the diligence of former collectors.

" At the decease of his son, (Edward Lord Harley, in 1741,) who had been a powerful auxiliary in enriching the collection, the MS. library consisted of nearly 8000 volumes. At the death of Mr. Harley, his library was bequeathed to the University of Oxford. To such men we owe a debt of gratitude for the improvement of the art and for introducing a style of finishing that still remains the admiration of the connoisseur.

" The books in the Harleian Collection are principally bound in red morocco, well sewed on raised bands, tight backs, (as were all the books of that period,) Dutch marble end-papers, and gilt edges."

Harleian tools are more wiry and much closer

than the Montague, interspersed with fine-line curls, fine pinhead curve-lines, rosettes, acorns, solid stops, single rings, and cross-buns.

The border upon the same plate illustrates the Harleian pane-side. In the Harleian style there are three distinctly different arrangements for sides and backs, (independent of the flights of fancy in which finishers indulge.) There are on the sides,— first, the two or three-line fillet, stopped; second, the Harleian tooled or spikey border,—a style of finishing peculiarly neat and rich, and well adapted for nearly every description of books.

On original Harleys the tooling went right on from corner to corner, as if worked by a very broad roll; but modern finishers prefer a made-up corner,—that is, a tool or tools projecting at right angles with the corner, up to which the border-tools are worked, thus rendering the whole more harmonious and perfect. The spikey border is worked up to a two or three-line fillet, with the cat-tooth roll worked on the outer line towards the edge of the board. (We may here mention that the cat-tooth, although purely French, may be also considered Harleian, as it is on all the originals we have seen, and accords well with the style.) Third, the pane or panelled side, similar to the illustration. Sometimes a double pane was formed by throwing in a two-line fillet and working a roll on the inside.

On the backs there is the upright centre, the diamond centre and corner, as in the illustration, and the semi-circle with open centre.

The diamond centre was not much used on books of light reading, such as novels, but rather on works of a graver nature, such as divinity, philosophy, and history. It seems to have been the favourite style of the earl's binders; and we must acknowledge that a book never looks so like a book as when finished with a good diamond centre and corner. In forming the diamond centre, the spikes ought to project beyond the stops, as it is then more graceful and pleasing to the eye than when the stop and spikes are flush one with the other.

THE FONTHILL STYLE.

The following account of Fonthill Abbey will, no doubt, be acceptable, in connection with our description of the " style" which has derived its name therefrom.

"Fonthill Abbey, in Wiltshire, justly ranks as one of the grandest structures in the United Kingdom, combining all the elegance of modern architecture with the sublime grandeur of the conventual

18

style. It was built about the end of the last
century, at an expense of £400,000, by Mr. William
Beckford, son of the public-spirited Lord Mayor of
London of that name, whose statue now stands in
Guildhall, with a copy of the memorable speech
and remonstrance which he addressed to George III.
in 1770. Succeeding to almost unbounded wealth,
(nearly £100,000 a year,) endowed with an extraordinary mind, literary talents of the highest order,
and an exquisite taste for the arts, the young owner
of Fonthill Abbey determined to erect an edifice
uncommon in design, and to adorn it with splendour; and, with an energy and enthusiasm of which
duller minds can form but a poor conception, he
soon had his determination carried into effect.

"The gorgeous edifice reared for Mr. B. contained
many magnificent suites of apartments. We need
only notice two, denominated St. Michael's, and
King Edward the Third's Gallery. They are of
the most stately and interesting description that
can be conceived or imagined: the former filled
with the choicest books and many articles of *vertu*;
the latter also employed as a library, but enriched
with a much greater number of choice and curious
productions, and terminating in an oratory, unique
for its elegant proportions and characteristic con-

sistency. It is at once rich and luxurious as the temple of which it forms an appendage,—sombre and soothing as the religious feelings with which its designation associates it.

&

> 'Meditation here may think down hours and moments;
> Here the heart may give a useful lesson to the head,
> And learning wiser grow without its books.'

It is but the drawing of a curtain, and not only all the glitter of the adjoining splendour, but all the pomps and vanities of the world seem to the meditative mind to be shut out forever. Perhaps its pensive cast is more deeply experienced from the immediate contrast: dazzled with objects of show, fatigued with the examination of rare and costly commodities, and bewildered with the multitude of precious devices which everywhere surround him, the soul of the visitant retires with tenfold delight to the narrow walls of the oratory."

Our brief description of the Fonthill style cannot fail to strike the reader as being remarkably appropriate to the sombre character of that part of the abbey which contained the library,—the one being in strict keeping with the other.

Half-bound olive-brown morocco; sewed on raised bands; gilt tops; marble-paper sides and insides;

with no finishing whatever, except the lettering and date at bottom.

À LA JANSENISTE.

This chaste and beautiful style is said to be derived from a religious order, and is highly esteemed by amateurs. Books bound à la janseniste are full-bound Turkey or Levant morocco, with a broad turn in on the inside of the board, gilt edges with a fine one-line fillet each side of the bands and head and tail, and neatly mitred on the side, all in blind, there being no gilding on the outside but the lettering; on the inside a broad-tooled border of very fine tooling in gold, a fine two-line in gold on the edges of the boards, and the cap of the headbands tipped with the same.

THE CAMBRIDGE STYLE

Is practised, we may say exclusively, on theological works. At what period it gained its name is uncertain; doubtless, it was the style in which some of the university libraries were chiefly bound; and, in all probability, the idea of the Harley paned side was first copied from it. Books bound in this style are sewed on raised bands, brown calf, pane-sprinkled sides, Dutch marble end-papers, and red

Modern Monastic.

edges. Back pieced with red russia, and a two-line fillet head and tail, and on each side of the bands, *blind*. Sides, two-line fillet close to the edge and on each side of the pane, with a narrow flower-roll worked on each side of the pane, close to the lines. The fillets in the pane to be connected together at the corners with the two-line fillet, and a tool worked from the corner of the pane towards the edge of the book, *all blind*. Bar-roll on the edges, in gold.

MODERNIZED MONASTIC.

This style is now in great vogue, under the appellation of the antique. The materials employed are divinity calf and brown or Carmelite morocco, with very thick boards, edges either red, brown, or matted gilt; very high raised bands. The style of ornament is illustrated by Plate II., intended for a side-stamp to be done by the press. It can also be done by hand, with rolls, fillets, and hand-stamps, omitting the broad and narrow fillet, and substituting either a one or two-line, working the circles with gouges. The tools are all worked blind. This style of binding, when appropriate to the book, produces a very pleasing effect.

18*

ARABESQUE.

" 'The term is more commonly applied to the species
of ornament used in adorning the walls, pavements,
and roofs of Moorish and Arabian buildings, consisting of an intricate heterogeneous admixture of
fruits, flowers, scrolls, and other objects, to the ex-
clusion of animals, the representation of which is
forbidden by the Mohammedan religion. This kind
of ornament is now frequently used in the adorning
of books, plate, &c. Foliage very similar to that
used by the Arabians, intermixed with griffins, &c.,
were frequently employed on the walls and friezes
of temples, and on many of the ancient Greek
vases; on the walls of the baths of Titus, at
Pompeii, and many other places."—*Craig's Universal Dictionary*.

As regards book-finishing, we have looked into
more than one authority, and are really unable to
define what the "arabesque" style is or ought to be.
The well-understood term "roan embossed" is, in
our opinion, the nearest approach to it at the
present day.

Plate III. is an adaptation of an old German
design for embossing. The figure is raised, the plate
being worked with a counter, in a powerful press.

Old German Style for Embossed Work

This style can only be executed upon publishers' work where there is a quantity of the same book to be done in this style. By it a good effect is produced upon an inferior material and at a trifling cost. The covers are embossed before they are applied to the volumes, and in order to preserve the sharpness of the design they must be covered with glue and not pressed afterwards.

ANTIQUE OAK AND OTHER BINDINGS.

Great varieties of style in the covers of bindings have been introduced within the last few years; but these must be left to the imitative powers of the skilful workman, as no written description would give the requisite information and guidance. Should he be desirous of executing these, he will do well to study some good specimen. Among others may be mentioned the Antique Oak Bindings, adopted by Mr. Murray, for his "Illuminated Prayer-Book," and Messrs. Longman and Co., for "Gray's Elegy." Also the Iron Binding,—viz.: covers in imitation of cast-iron,—in which Messrs. Longman and Co. have had bound the "Parables of our Lord." Bibles and Prayers are now frequently bound to imitate the antique, having heavy boards with clasps and corners, and finished in the monastic style.

GROLIER STYLE.

This beautiful style of ornament is so well illustrated by Plate IV. that it scarcely needs any remark. We will merely observe that this style is well calculated for hand-work, being entirely superficial in character. The pattern presented can be worked with a one-line fillet and gouges, with a few leaves of a conventional character. The design should be first traced upon paper of the proper size, the paper lightly tipped at the corners with paste upon the side, then worked with the fillet and gouges through the paper upon the leather. The paper is then removed, and the blind impression appears upon the side. All vestiges of the paper are carefully washed off, and the pattern pencilled in,—that is, each portion of the figure is carefully traced with a fine camel's-hair pencil saturated with glaire. When dry it is lightly passed over with a piece of cotton in which sweet oil has been dropped, and the gold leaf laid on. The pattern is then reworked upon the gold.

The design upon Plate V. is a modern elaboration of the Grolier, and is intended for a side-plate,

Grolier about 1530

.

Modernized Grolier

  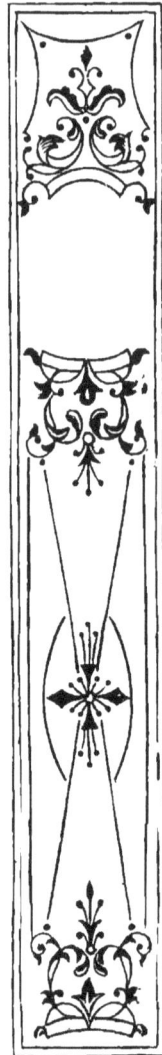

Louis XIV.　　　　Modern　　　　French

Drawn after a design by Holbein A. D. 1550.

to be executed by the stamping-press. It is well calculated for blind or blank stamping, the solid line producing by its intersections a fine effect. By omitting the inner and working the out lines, this elaboration of lines and circles can be worked by hand.

The Louis Quatorze is illustrated, by a pattern for a back, upon Plate VI. This can be worked either by hand-stamps or by the press. The centre pattern is a very pretty illustration of the prevailing style of backs for case-work. This must be stamped before the cover is applied to the book.

The third pattern for flat backs is adapted for hand-tools, and when executed upon light-coloured English calf produces a beautiful appearance. From its light, graceful character, it is well suited to modern poetry and light literature in general. This style gives scope to an almost endless variety of patterns, regulated only by the taste of the finisher.

Plate VII. is a design drawn by Holbein for a side-ornament in metal. This beautiful pattern can be adapted either to hand or press work. Its graceful and harmonious proportions should be well studied by the young workman.

Upon Plate VIII. will be found specimens of rolls and hand-stamps used in finishing. The num-

bers affixed refer to the order of arrangement in
the Book of Patterns published by Gaskill, Copper
& Fry, containing over two thousand specimens
with their prices attached. They have also an immense number of patterns, executed since the publication of their book for binders in various parts
of the country.

Having given the prominent distinct styles,—of
which there are, however, many combinations, both
of style, ornament, and tooling, originating more
nondescripts than we have space to treat upon,—
we proceed to the gilding, trusting that what has
been pointed out to the attention of the young
workman will induce him to neglect no opportunities
of becoming acquainted with the works of artists of
celebrity, not for the purpose of servile imitation,
but to examine their adaptations of ornamental art
as a study, to enable him to trace superficial decoration back to its originators. Having acquired this
knowledge, he may by his treatment of ornament
take rank as an artist.

The examples given will be sufficient for the in-
tellectual workman to conceive many patterns
which his taste will suggest, forming an infinite
variety of beautiful designs. In all combinations,
a rigorous observance of the symmetrical propor-

Selection from Gaskill, Copper & Fry's Book of Patterns

tions of the tools must be his first care, so that the
union of any number of designs present a form
agreeable and chaste. It would be superfluous to
add more; but from the importance of the subject,
on closing the directions for the ornamental department of binding, it may be repeated that there is
no greater evidence of the ignorance or carelessness
of the workman than an ornament of any kind
unevenly or unequally worked. Let the young
binder especially bear this in mind: it is a defect
which nothing can effectually remedy; instead of
an embellishment it is a detriment to the binding,
and his reputation as a clever workman is consequently placed in jeopardy.

Preparatory to gilding, the back must be com-
passed off and carefully marked with a folding-stick
and a straight-edge or piece of vellum, wherever it
is intended to run a straight line. This serves as a
guide when the gold is laid on. For work of the
best class, the fillets must be first put in blind, and
the tooling done in the same manner. For sides
where the design is elaborate, or a degree of perfection in the tooling is desirable, the entire pattern
must be first worked in blind, and, after being
washed with a dilution of oxalic acid or a thin paste-
wash, it must be carefully pencilled in with the

glaire-pencil; but this comes more appropriately
under the head of

PREPARATIONS FOR GILDING.

To operate successfully, it will be necessary that
the workman provide himself with good size, glaire,
and oil. The first is prepared by boiling fine vellum
slips till a good size is produced, of a consistency
that will lie equally on the volume without blotches
or ropes, and must be used warm. The glaire is
formed of the whites of eggs, beaten well with a
frother till it is perfectly clear, and the froth taken
ɔff. This liquid will improve by keeping, and
should never be used new if it can possibly be
avoided. For morocco bindings, the glaire is sometimes diluted with water. The oil adopted by
various binders is different. Some use palm-oil for
calf, sweet oil for morocco or russia; others prefer
hog's lard, or fine mould-candle, for light-coloured
calf; but sweet oil is well adapted for almost every
kind of leather. Vellum-size is the best preparation for coloured calf. On books thus prepared,
the glaire must be applied two or three times, taking
care that each coat is quite dry before the next is
added, and that it lies perfectly even on the whole
surface, free from globules or any substance what-

ever. Great care is required in preparing coloured calf; for, if there be too much body in the preparation, it will crack on the surface and present a bad appearance. Morocco and roan will not require more than one coat, and, where practicable, only on such parts of the morocco as are to be gilt. The state of the weather must ever determine the number of volumes to be proceeded with at one time, as in the winter double the number may be glaired to what the dryness of a summer's day will admit of, so as to work with safety and produce effect. A good paste-wash before glairing is always advisable, as it prevents the glaire from sinking into the leather.

In preparing glaire from the egg for immediate use, a few drops of oxalic acid added thereunto will be found to be of essential service.

The volumes being thus prepared, the operation of

GILDING THE BACK

Is commenced by oiling slightly, with a small piece of cotton, the whole length of the back. If the book is merely intended to be *filleted* for the economy of the gold, small strips are cut on the gold-cushion, attached to the heated fillet by rolling it slightly over, and affixed to the volume by passing it firmly

19

on the lines previously marked. But if the back is
to be fully ornamented, it will be necessary to cover
it entirely with gold-leaf.

The hand-stamps should be disposed on the table
before him, so as to be selected with the greatest
facility, and in readiness for every purpose for
which they may be required.

To lay on the gold, the workman takes a book of
the metal, opens the outside leaf, and passes the
knife underneath the gold; with this he raises it,
carries it steadily on to the cushion, and spreads it
perfectly even, by a light breath on the middle of
the leaf, taking care also that not the least current
of air has access to the room he may be operating
in. Afterwards the gold must be cut with the gold-
knife to the breadth and length of the places to be
covered, by laying the edge upon˙ it and moving
the knife slightly backwards and forwards. Then
rub upon the back the oil, and apply the gold upon
the places to be ornamented with a cotton or tip,
rubbed on the forehead or hair to give it a slight
humidity and cause the gold to adhere. But if the
whole of the back is to be gilt, it will be more economical to entirely cover it by cutting the gold
in slips the breadth of the book and applying
the back on it; afterwards press it close with the

cotton, with which any breaks in the gold must also
be covered, by placing small slips where required.
The humidity of the hair or forehead will be sufficient to make the gold adhere to the cotton or
other instrument with which it may be conveyed to
the book.   The fillet or roll must then be heated to
a degree proper for the substance on which it is to
be worked.   Calf will require them hotter than morocco and roan, and these warmer than russia and
vellum.   To ascertain their proper heat, they are
applied on a damp sponge, or rubbed with the finger
wetted, and by the degree of boiling that the water
makes, their fitness is known; but a little exercise
and habit will render this easy of judging.   To
further insure this, the roll or pallet is passed over
the cap of the headband; if too hot, the gold will
be dull; if too cool, the impression will be bad,
from the gold not adhering in every part.

After the gold is laid on, the volume is laid upon
the side, with the back elevated, and the workman
proceeds to mitre the fillets that run lengthwise of
the back, commencing at the line that has been
traced across the back, by pressing lightly with the
point of the mitred roll and running it carefully
till near the line that marks the end of the panel;
then lift the fillet and turn it with the finger until

the other or reverse mitre, or nick in the fillet, is
reached; then place the fillet in the lines already
gilt, adjusting it with the left hand until the extreme
point of the mitre will just reach the line traced
across.   After both edges of the back have been
done along the joint in this way, the volume is then
placed evenly in the finishing-press, and the panels
completed by mitreing the fillets that run across the
back.   The entire operation requires the utmost
care, in order to have the lines parallel and the
mitres perfectly even and true.   No ornament that
may be afterwards worked upon the back, beautiful
as it may be, can atone for negligence or want of
skill in the mitreing and running of the fillets.   As
a matter of economy, sometimes the back is run up;
that is, instead of stopping where the lines or bands
intersect, the roll is run up the back from one end
to the other, without stopping; and, after wiping
the gold off along the joint outside the fillet, it is
run across the back on each side of the bands, and
head and tail in the same manner.   After the back
is mitred, the finisher will proceed with the ornamental tools, and work them carefully off.   In
placing them, great attention should be paid to their
occupying precisely the same place in each panel :
and, in order to present an agreeable effect, the

tools should correspond in detail, and there should be a geometrical fitness governing the selection and arrangement of the tools.

The judicious choice of ornaments for the back is of the utmost importance. For instance, such as represent animals, insects, or flowers, which are only proper for works of natural history, entomology, and botany, should never appear on the backs of works on general literature, as it would be an evidence of bad taste or carelessness.

Every tool should be beautiful in itself, because no accumulation of misshapen tools can make one beautiful ornament. There is no objection to scrolls, leaves, flowers, stops, or any of the usual kind of ornaments; only let them all be in themselves beautiful. It is appropriate to introduce a harp on a book of songs, a stag's head on a book on hunting, a recognised ecclesiastical pattern upon a book of divinity or a prayer-book; a Greek or Roman design upon a classical work, or a Gothic design upon a book on Gothic architecture.

Should it be desired to present on the back simply an ornamental lettering-piece at the head, diverging to a point towards the middle of the book, and the rest of the volume left plain, it will be necessary to impress the tools previous to glairing, and then apply

19*

the glaire with a camel's-hair pencil in the indentations the tools have formed. When dry, cover with
gold and reimpress the tool in the marks previously
made, and letter the title. This proceeding is
adopted in every pattern where part of the back is
intended to be left dull by being free from glaire.

The title must next engage attention, and the
letters placed thereon, either singly or together,
with brass type properly fixed in the hand-chase.
If with single letters, the tail of the volume must
be lowered about an inch, and the workman draw a
thread of silk across the gold to direct the heads of
the letters. Taking each singly, he places them on
the back with the right hand, steadying the letter
with the forefinger of the left. If the title is set in
the chase, place the volume evenly in the press, and
apply the title, guided by the thumb, firmly across.
The title in either case must be justified, to produce
the best effect, taking care to avoid, if possible,
having two lines of the same length; and, where the
title can be measured, as in the type it may, the
exact centre should be ascertained before applying
it heated on the gold. The back may now be considered finished. The gold which has not been impressed by the gilding tools must be well rubbed off
with the *gold-rag* and minutely cleared off with a

piece of fine flannel or India-rubber, so as to display the delicate lines of the ornaments as perfectly and clearly as possible. Attention should be paid to this particular; for, let a book be finished in the most tasteful manner possible, unless well cleared off the effect is entirely lost. If in calf, it must now be polished, and the squares and edges of the boards proceeded with.

GILDING THE SQUARES, ETC.

For gilding the edges of the boards, the gold may be taken as for the bands,—on the roll,—and the volume held firmly with the left hand; but, if large, put into the press between boards, so as not to injure the back. Where the ornament of the inside-square is simple, the like proceeding of applying the gold will be proper, resting the board open on an elevation equal to the thickness of the book. But if the square has been left large, with a leather joint, so as to admit of being more elaborately filled up, the gold must be laid on the whole space with the tip and pressed close with the cotton. The gilding is then proceeded with in the same manner as detailed in the directions for the side-ornaments.

GILDING THE SIDES.

The sides, from affording more ample space, are
the part of the volume whereon the workman can
and is expected to show his taste and skill in gilding.
The proceedings are the same as before pointed out
where a simple roll is the only ornament round;
but where the pattern is extensive and the details
minute, it is necessary to have the whole worked
blind upon the volume before glairing, and then
apply the gold. If one side is done at a time, the
book is taken by the leaves with the left hand, the
board intended to be covered resting on the thumb,
and the gold laid on as for the squares, either over
the whole side or on such parts as the pattern indi-
cates. If the volume be small, the gold may be
laid on both sides and the leaves of the volume
placed in the finishing-press, allowing the boards to
rest on its surface. This affords greater facility for
placing uniformly and systematically the fillets, rolls,
and tools necessary to complete the design on each
side. Where the pattern has not been marked, and
one side only proceeded with, the roll is run in a
straight line, which should be made, previous to
covering with gold, on the board by the joint of the
back, the volume turned for the head and tail, and

laid open upon the board for the fore-edge, to give it the firmness necessary.

Directions for executing the most elaborate designs have been previously given, whereby it will be perceived that it requires but taste, and a just observation of similarity of design and the geometrical proportions of the ornaments, to execute them to any extent. One variation from this rule will destroy the effect of the whole pattern : it will therefore be to the benefit of such as are not conversant fully with the art, to assist themselves with designs drawn on cartridge-paper, which may be marked through on the leather and the pattern executed in gold or blind as required. In all, the gilding will be the same, either to glaire over the whole cover after the design is stamped, or, if the plain part is to be left dull, by glairing the impressions only with a camel's-hair pencil.

GILDING ON SILK AND VELVET.

The proceedings necessary to be adopted for gilding on silk and velvet are, from the delicate nature of these substances, different from those laid down for gilding on leather. The glaire used on the latter would tend to stain, and therefore it is necessary to employ other means for fixing the gold.

This is by drying the whites of eggs and reducing
them to a powder, which is put into a small bottle
and tightly tied over with a piece of fine muslin,
by which means it is equally distributed on the
space intended to be gilt. Gum-sandarac is now,
however, more generally used for this purpose,
although some use gum-copal. The powder being
applied, the gold is cut in slips and taken on a roll
of a circumference equal to the length of the space
intended for it to be applied on. The design is then
firmly impressed, and the superfluous gold brushed
off with a soft brush or clean piece of cotton, and
the other side alike executed. In lettering, or
fixing single tools on the back, the same proceedings
must be adopted, by taking the gold thereon and
applying it to the back or side of the volume.
Where the design is large, or elaborate work is required, it will be better executed in the following
manner :—The design must be drawn on paper, and
worked through on silk, after which the impression
must be carefully glaired with a camel's-hair pencil;
when dry, rub the parts intended for the gold with
the finger passed through the hair or with a clean
rag slightly oiled, and, after laying on the gold as
directed for other styles, reimpress the tools, and
whip off the superfluous gold with a clean flannel.

As there is no moisture in silk, the workman must not lay on at one time so much as he does on calf and other substances.

ILLUMINATED BINDING.

This style, an invention of the French, was for some time kept by them with the greatest secrecy. It is a binding of the utmost magnificence, uniting the varied beauties of the arabesque and gilt ornament, blended with the illuminated decorations seen on early MSS. before the invention of printing. When executed in the best manner, nothing can exceed the beauty of the whole *coup-d'œil*, rivalling, as it does, in splendour, the most elaborately-finished design of the painter. The time required to be devoted, on its first introduction, to a single specimen, appeared likely to confine this sort of ornament to the finest treasures of literature, and even to them in a limited degree. The improvements, however, in machinery and the rapid advance of the arts have, in a few years, brought this style into very general use for albums and other works where embellished covers are adopted; and even on the cheap roan bindings used for Bibles, Prayers, &c. it may be seen; though in effecting this cheapness it must be premised that a less durable method is adopted.

To execute the more elaborate designs, practice and a taste for the arts will here alone serve the workman; without these requisites it would be futile to make the attempt. But, as the proceedings require to be executed with the utmost care, we shall enter fully into such as are new, and, from their importance, at the risk of being considered prolix, again touch on those that may have been before treated of.

The description of one side will serve the purpose of making the proceedings fully understood. Whether the material be of morocco or white vellum, it must be washed, if required, perfectly clean, and left to dry. The first operation will be—if it be for stamp-work—to place the side on the bed of the stamping-press and boldly impress the design thereon. The most elegant, and capable of the greatest display of colour, are subjects of botany and natural history. The next step will be to glaire with a camel's-hair pencil such parts of the impression as it is intended shall be afterwards covered with gold. This done, the delicate operation of colouring may be proceeded with. In London and Paris this is executed by professed artists in no way conversant with book-binding. The colours to be used must be such as do not at all, or very slightly, fade on exposure to the air or sun, such as carmine, ultramarine, indigo, burnt sienna, gamboge, and sap-green. These must be prepared, with fine gum, in the same manner as for painting, and be lightly and delicately laid on such parts of the design as it is intended the colour should occupy, taking care that the ground-colour or leather is entirely hid. Let every thing be true to nature, each bird, plant, and flower its proper colour, and a general harmony prevail throughout. When finished, let the whole perfectly dry, and then, in the manner directed, lay gold on such parts as it is intended, in the reimpression of the plate, should be further embellished. Heat the plate, place the side again under it, and give it a firm and sharp impression. Rub off the superfluous gold, and the whole of the delicate lines of the ornament will be found beautifully gilt, the colours firmly fixed by the heat of the plate, and the rough edges of the colour completely effaced by the reimpression of the original design.

In executing the less expensive and more simple designs, the plate is impressed in gold on the side, and the parts left ungilt on the leather; afterwards coloured according to the taste of the workman.

For the best class of work, after the design is impressed, either by hand or the press, pieces are

20

cut out of variously-coloured morocco, pared thin,
and neatly pasted on the side, the design, when
worked, entirely concealing the edges of the morocco. This is termed inlaid work.

BLIND TOOLING.

This is an ornamental operation, applied either
before or after the book has been gilt and polished,
and, if judiciously intermingled with the gold, will
not fail to present a good effect. It is a style that
has been much used of late years, and is executed
in the same way and with the same tools as for gilding, but without any gold applied on the places thus
ornamented. The rolls, pallets, and smaller tools,
are applied by the hand, and the large plates with
the press, with the same precautions as indicated in
the previous section. If the pattern consists of
straight lines, and the workman possesses a good
eye, the best manner of executing it is by making
use of a pallet, placing it firmly on the book, and
sliding it to the opposite point. It remains, therefore, to consider such matters as more immediately
apply to this style of decoration.

The tools for blind tooling should not be so warm
as for gilding, and particularly for morocco. If it
is wished to be left dull,—that is, free from glaire,—

the particles attaching themselves over the edge of the gold ornaments must be removed with the end of the finger, wrapped over with a piece of fine cloth, and wetted. This will soon wash it clean, and when dry the blind ornaments may be proceeded with.

Graining may be properly considered as a blind ornament. This is where, by the means of wooden or metal plates, the sides of a book are marked with lines crossed over each other, so as to form innumerable small squares in imitation of russia, or in imitation of the grain of morocco, scales of fish, and other substances. The operation is performed by placing the volume between the two plates even by the groove of the back, in the standing-press, and pressing it tightly down, and so even that the plate will be impressed equally over the whole surface. Nothing will look worse than a bold impression in one place and a slight one in another; and therefore it becomes of importance to see that it is evenly pressed, as a second application of some kind of plates will never be found affixed to the same places.

MODERNIZED MONASTIC OR ANTIQUE.

This style, whether done by the hand or the press, is one that requires care and patience on the part

of the workman, so as to bring up the tools black,
without burning or otherwise injuring the leather.
We have spent much, time in experiments, so as to
arrive at the most certain and perfect mode of producing the desired result. The style emanated from
Mr. Hayday's bindery; and a volume executed in
this style for a connoisseur in this city, with tooling of a brilliant black, fell into our hands some
years since, and we at once set about attempting to
produce the same effects. Our efforts were confined
to hand-tooling for some time; and, although inferior
in effect, they were generally well received; but we
were far from being satisfied. We tried every substance that could be thought of, made the leather
and tools hot and dry, or wet and cold, as reason
seemed to point to one or the other as the proper
method. We will now communicate the results of
our labours :—In the first place, the material is of
the greatest importance; and the finest effects cannot be produced except upon English calf or morocco. American calf is entirely out of the question
for the purpose, as the morocco is too hard on the
surface, and there is not sufficient colour in the
body for the tools to draw and affix it by heat to
the surface; but some kinds are better adapted for
the purpose than others. To test this, apply the

tip of the tongue to the leather, and if the dampness lies on the surface, without sinking in, reject
it ; but if the dampness strikes instantly into the
leather,—the quicker the better,—the workman may
proceed with some hopes of success. After the
volume is covered and ready for finishing, wash it
evenly over with clean water; and, as soon as the
water ceases to lie upon the surface, apply the tool
moderately heated; this will bring up the dark
colour. Afterwards go over it again with the tool, so
as to make the impressions clear and bright. There
are, however, some colours, as well as particular
manufactures, that will not come up black ; and we
were long satisfied that some colouring-matter
was employed. We wrote to a friend in London,
who sent us the material and the method of its use.
The material was common printers' ink. His com-
munication we now make public. " In the first
place, the leather should be quite damp, and the tools
used should be as hot as possible without the printers'
ink. Then again impressed with the printers' ink
upon the tools. We put the larger tools in again
without ink. When the ink is used upon the tools,
the leather should be rather damp, and the tools not
very hot. When the pattern is worked in the manner described, it should be left until dry, and then
20*

brushed with a brush, not very stiff, which will give
a brilliant gloss to the tooling." When using
printers' ink, be careful not to get too much on the
tools.

Let the young workman but follow the directions
given, and, with a little patience and reflection, he
will be able to do work of the character under consideration, fully equal to the efforts of the best
workman, provided that the tools be worked true
and even.

POLISHING.

The details of this operation, which is performed
immediately after the gold ornaments have been
worked, have been reserved in order that the whole
of the ornamental department might be kept
together. Morocco, roan, silk, and velvet, and the
blind ornaments on any substance, must never be
submitted to the action of the polisher. A smart
rubbing with a piece of rough calf will be sufficient
for the two former, and the velvet or silk will merely
require cleaning with any smooth substance or with
India-rubber.

There are two polishers,—one for the back and
bands, and another for the sides. The oil applied
on the cover previous to laying on the gold will be

2

[R5]

ART OF BOOKBINDING. 235

sufficient to make the polisher glide easily over the surface. The polisher must be heated, and well cleaned on a board, and passed quickly and evenly on the back, sides, or joints, as the case may be, taking especial care that it is not too hot, as the glaire would thereby be turned white and the work damaged in appearance, nor so cold as to give a bad polish.

The book, as gilt, must be first polished on the back, by taking it with the left hand, resting it on the table, and polished with the right hand by gliding backwards and forwards the smooth part of the polisher on the whole extent of the back. This not only polishes the surface, but smooths down the indentations formed upon the leather by the gilding-tools, bringing up the gilding to the surface. The polisher must be passed on such places only as it is wished to make brilliant, and great care taken not to touch the places intended to be left dull.

The sides are similarly polished, by laying the volume on the table, covered with baize, and passing the large iron quickly over, first from the fore-edge towards the groove, and then, by turning the volume in a contrary way, from the tail to the head.

If the joint requires polishing, the book is laid before the workman, the tail towards him, and the iron applied on the side next the groove, polishing the whole length of the board; then, turning round the volume, and bringing the fore-edge towards him, he polishes the side on the fore-edge, and, turning again, completes the whole by polishing the parts at the head and tail.

In addition to polishing, it is desirable to give to the sides the greatest possible smoothness by pressing them between polished tins or horns. These are placed on each side of the book even by the groove, put between pressing-boards, and screwed tightly in the press, and left for some time.

COLOURING.

Calf-skins of uniform tints, and also sprinkled, can now be obtained of English manufacturers; yet in many localities they are difficult to obtain. We therefore make known the chemical substances and ingredients required to execute them in the best manner. Marbling is a process that must be executed by the binder upon the cover, and, with many other revival styles, is again coming into vogue. The recipes given for the superior marbles and designs will, it is presumed, present this branch of the art on a higher footing, in a general point of view, than is usually accorded to it; and it is confidently asserted that not one of them will prove a failure, if attention to the directions be only given. Nothing has been omitted in the description of the substances best for use, the mode of preparing them, and the proceedings to be adopted, that can tend to give to the covers all the elegance and splendour of which they are susceptible. By the aid of these, assisted by some taste, the workman may vary the designs almost to infinity; but it must be admitted that, unless he is devoted to his art, no mere directions or casual advantages will enable him to succeed in the more complicated or delicate operations, while, with an ardour for it, all difficulties will be easily overcome.

CHEMICAL PREPARATIONS.

Under this head is included *aqua regii*, or killed spirits, *nitric acid*, *marbling-water*, and *glaire* prepared for marbling.

AQUA REGII,

So called from its power to dissolve gold, is a mixture of nitrous acid (aquafortis) and muriatic acid, (spirits of salts,) deprived of its burning qualities by block-tin, which it dissolves. It is called by the chemist *acid nitro-muriatic:* the muriatic also contains a portion of alkali, which gives to red a vinous tint, and for which colour it is principally used.

The two substances should be of the purest quality, of a concentration of thirty-three degrees for the nitric acid and of twenty degrees for the muriatic. They must be mixed with the greatest precaution. Having provided a clear glass bottle, the neck rather long, capable of holding twice the quantity to be prepared, place it upon a bed of sand, the opening at top, and pour in *one part* of pure nitric acid and *three* of muriatic. Let the first vapours dispel, and then cover the orifice with a small phial, which must not confine the vapour too closely, as the bottle would be liable to burst, but which retains as much as possible without risk. Of block-tin, an eighth part of the weight of the acid must then be dropped into the bottle, in small pieces, a little at a time, covering the orifice with the phial. The acid will immediately attack the tin and dissolve it, when a second portion must be put in with the same precaution, and so on till the whole is dissolved. *Malacca* tin is the best for use, and if pure there will be no sediment; but, as it cannot always be obtained, a black sediment will be left. The vapour having ceased, the acid must be poured into bottles and secured with glass stoppers, to preserve it. When used, a part is taken and mixed with *one quarter* of its weight of distilled water.

It is usual with some workmen to perform this operation in a common drinking-glass; but, as the vapour is thereby all dispersed, the composition loses a considerable portion of its best quality, for it will be observed, if performed in a bottle as above directed, that the vapour assumes a red tint, which does not escape if the neck of the bottle be of sufficient length.

ANOTHER.

Some binders adopt the following method; but, as it is not capable of producing an equal beauty and clearness of colour with the one above given, it will not be advisable to use. The former, too, will be equally effective to an indefinite period, while this will not preserve more than two or three months.

Put in a brown freestone pot two ounces of powdered *sal-ammoniac*, six ounces of fine *Malacca tin*, in strips or drops, twelve ounces of distilled water, and, last, a pound of *nitric acid*, of thirty-three degrees. Leave the whole till the tin is dissolved, and then pour off and bottle as above directed.

VITRIOL-WATER.

Vitriol, as sold in the pure state, will not be proper to use in marbling or sprinkling, as it would corrode and destroy the leather. It must be weakened at least in proportion of one ounce of vitriol to three of water.

MARBLING-WATER.

It is usual with many to use the water pure ; but a few drops of *potash liquid* mixed with it will be found to produce better effect, the marble being rendered more distinct.

GLAIRE.

Put spirits of wine in a proportion of two drops to the whites of twelve eggs, and beat the whole well together till perfectly clear.

PREPARATIONS OF THE COLOURS.

The preparations used by different binders vary much, as will be seen by the recipes given for the same colours, which we judge necessary to put on record, that nothing connected with the subject should be omitted, premising that each colour may be depended upon for producing the most satisfactory results. It may be proper also to observe that the whole of the woods and other ingredients used should be previously powdered or reduced to small pieces, the colours being thereby much better extracted.

BLACK.

1. Dissolve half a pound of green copperas in two quarts of water. The oxide contained in the sulphate of iron will combine with the tanning of the leather, and produce a good black.

2. Boil in a cast-iron pot a quart of vinegar, with a quantity of rusty nails, or steel-filings, till reduced one-third, taking off the scum as it rises to the top. This liquid improves by age. To keep up the quantity, boil with more vinegar.

3. A cheaper liquid may be produced by boiling two pints of beer and two pints of water with two pounds of old iron and a pint of vinegar, scumming as before, and bottling for use.

BROWN.

1. Half a pound of good Dantzic or American potash dissolved in one quart of rain-water, and preserved in a bottle well corked.

2. Salts or oil of tartar, in the same proportions as above.

21

3. A beautiful brown may be procured from the green shells of walnuts. To prepare this, a quantity of the green shells, when the nuts are gathered, must be pounded in a mortar to extract the juice, and then put into a vessel capable of holding a sufficient quantity of water. The water being put in, the whole should be frequently stirred, and left to soak, with the vessel covered. Afterwards the liquid must be passed through a sieve, the juice well expressed, and bottled, with some common salt, for use. This liquid, after fermentation, will produce the best effects for the uniform tints, as it tends to soften the leather, and will not corrode.

BLUE.

1. It is usual with many binders to use *Scott's Liquid Blue*, but it is necessary to know the preparation of the colour. Perhaps the best and most simple one known is one given by *Poerner*, which is as follows:—In four ounces of sulphuric acid, of 66 degrees, mix gradually one ounce of finely-powdered indigo, so as to form a sort of pulp. Place the vessel in another containing boiling water, for some hours, and then leave it to cool. Afterwards put to it a small portion of good potash, dry and finely powdered, stirring the whole well, and letting it rest

for twenty-four hours, when bottled, and use as required.   This colour will appear nearly black, but
may be made to any shade by adding water to it.
If any portion remain after being diluted, it must
be put into a separate bottle, as if mixed with the
first preparation the whole would be deteriorated.

2. A readier blue may be prepared by mixing
one ounce of powdered indigo with two ounces of
oil of vitriol, and letting it stand for twenty-four
hours, and then adding twelve ounces of pure water.

PURPLE.

Boil half a pint of archill or logwood with vinegar
and water, of each half a pint.

LILAC.

Same as for the purple, with the addition of about
two table-spoonsful of potash.

VIOLET.

Half a pound of logwood chips and one ounce of
Brazil dust, boiled over a good fire in four pints of
water till reduced one-half, and left to clear.   Then
throw in one ounce of powdered alum and two
grains of cream of tartar, and again boil till dissolved.   This liquid must be used warm.

FAWN.

In two pints of water boil one ounce of tan, and a like portion of nutgall, till reduced to a pint.

YELLOW.

1. To one ounce of good caked saffron, turmeric, or French berries, add a portion of spirits of wine or *aqua regii*, and leave the mixture to macerate. This liquid is used cold, and may be varied to any shade by adding water when required.

2. In two pints of water put eight ounces of French berries, and boil till reduced one-half. Then pass it through a sieve or fine cotton, and add a small quantity of powdered alum, and again boil, using it warm.

OHANGE.

In a pint and a half of potash liquid, boil a quarter of a pound of fustic chips till reduced one-half; then put in an ounce of good *annatto*, well beaten, and, after boiling, a small portion of alum, and use warm.

GREEN.

1. Liquid blue and yellow mixed will best suit for general purposes.

2. Dissolve in a bottle one ounce of verdigris in

an ounce of white wine vinegar, and place the whole before a fire for four or five days, frequently shaking the bottle.

RED.

There are three sorts of red,—viz.: common, fine, and scarlet.

Common.—1. In a tinned kettle boil half a pound of Brazil wood, eight grains of nutgalls, both powdered, and three pints of water, till the whole is reduced one-third. Then add powdered alum and sal-ammoniac, of each one ounce, and when dissolved strain through a sieve. This liquid must always be used warm.

2. Boil a quarter of a pound of Brazil dust, two ounces of powdered cochineal, and a little alum, in two pints of the best vinegar, till a bright red is produced. Use warm.

Fine.—1. In three pints of water boil half a pound of Brazil dust and half an ounce of powdered nutgalls. Pass the whole through a fine cotton, and replace the liquid on the fire, adding one ounce of powdered alum and half an ounce of sal-ammoniac. Give the whole another boil, and then add a portion of *aqua regii*, according to the shade desired, and use warm.

2. A quicker and cheaper proceeding is by putting in a cup a portion of Brazil wood, and adding to it

21*

the *aqua regii*, letting it stand for a quarter of an hour to extract the colour.

Scarlet.—To one ounce of white nutgalls and one ounce of cochineal, both finely powdered, add two pints of boiling water. After boiling some time, add half an ounce of *aqua regii*, and use warm.

MARBLING.

Before proceeding to a description of the marbles, and other designs on the covers coming under the general head of marbling, it will be proper to give a few directions relative to some important matters required in the way of preparation. As the success of many of the designs depends upon the quickness with which they are executed, it will be important that the colours, sponges, brushes, &c. are previously disposed in the best order, so as to be of the readiest access. Attention should be paid to the probable quantity that may be required of each colour, as many of them will not be available for use another time.

The books should all be previously washed with paste and water to which has been added a little pearlash liquid, and left to dry. After this they must be glaired equally over, and when dry placed upon the marbling-rods, the sides of the books extending over and the leaves hanging between. The rods must be placed on an elevation at the top, so as to allow the water to run gradually towards the bottom of the books; and, if the backs are required to be left plain, another rod, or piece of board, grooved to the shape of the back, placed on them. To avoid the scum arising from the beating of the brushes over the colours, it is better to rub the ends of the bristles on the palm of the hand, on which a little oil has been spread. These preliminaries being settled, the operation of marbling commences, for which we shall now give directions.

COMMON MARBLE.

The book being placed on the rods, throw on the water prepared for marbling in large drops, with a coarse brush, or bunch of quills, till the drops unite. Then, with a brush charged with the black liquid and beaten on the press-pin as directed for sprinkling the edges, a number of fine streaks are produced by throwing the colour equally over the cover. Afterwards the brown liquid must be similarly thrown over. When the veins are well struck into the leather, the water must be sponged off and the book placed to dry.

If the volume has been previously coloured with any of the preparations before described, and it is wished to produce a marble thereon, the brown must be thrown on first, and then the black; as without this precaution the marble would not strike, because of the acid which forms part of the colours. This observation being applicable to all the other designs, it will not be necessary again to repeat it.

ANOTHER.

Throw on the vinegar-black, then the brown, and lastly a sprinkle of vitriol-water.

PURPLE MARBLE.

Colour the cover two or three times with hot purple liquid, and, when dry, glaire. Then throw on water, and sprinkle with strong vitriol-water, which will form red veins.

STONE MARBLE.

After throwing on the water, sprinkle boldly with the black liquid; then, with a sponge charged with strong brown, drop the colour on the back in three or four places, so that it may run down each side in a broad stream, and afterwards operate with vitriol-water on the parts the brown has not touched.

GREEN AGATE.

Sprinkle black, in nine times its quantity of water, in large drops over the whole surface of the cover, and when the drops unite apply on the back at regular distances the green liquid, so that it may flow on the boards and unite with the black.

BLUE AGATE.

Proceed as above, only substituting blue in place of the green, weakened with water according to the shade required.

FAIR AGATE.

Commence by sprinkling black in small drops at a good distance from each other; afterwards sprinkle equally over large drops of weak potash.

AGATINE.

Proceed as for the green agate, and then sprinkle scarlet all over the cover; finally, throw on blue in small drops, weakened in four times the quantity of water.

LEVANT MARBLE.

After the water, throw on the back-brown in broad streaks as directed for the *stone*, and then in

like manner the *aqua regii*.   This will be found to
imitate closely the Levant marble.

PORPHYRY VEIN.

Throw on large drops of black diluted in double
the quantity of water.   When the colour has struck
well into the leather, sprinkle in the same manner
brown mixed equally with water.   Then apply a
sprinkle of scarlet, and afterwards large spots of
yellow, the liquid nearly boiling.   While these
colours are uniting, throw on weak blue, and then
aqua regii, which, flowing together down the sides
of the book, will form the vein distinctly.

RED PORPHYRY.

Sprinkle with black in eight times the quantity
of water, very equal and in small spots.   Let it
dry, rub, and glaire.   Then give two or three
sprinkles of fine red, and one of scarlet, and again
leave to dry.   Finally, sprinkle scarlet in small
spots as equally as possible.

GREEN PORPHYRY.

For this design the cover must be finely sprinkled
over three separate times, leaving the colour to
search and dry between each.   The green must be

brought to the shade required by mixing with water. To form a more elegant vein, sprinkle first with weak black, and afterwards with green, and when dry with fine red.

PORPHYRY.

This marble, imitating the *eye of the partridge*, is executed by throwing on black in eight times its volume of water, in small drops, but so close as to just run into each other. When the black begins to flow, sprinkle over brown mixed equally with water. Let it dry, wash the whole with a sponge, and before quite dry again give it two or three coats of fine red. After being dry and well rubbed, sprinkle equally over the surface large drops of *aqua regii.*

ANOTHER.

Colour the cover with red, yellow, blue, or green, and, when dry, with black diluted as above; let this also dry, and then sprinkle over large or small drops of aqua regii. The eye of the partridge is properly formed with blue sprinkled upon the weakened black, and, when dry, with the killed spirit or *aqua regii.*

ROCK.

Throw on large drops of black prepared as for the porphyry, and, when half dry, weakened potash in the same manner. When dry again, sprinkle on equally small spots of scarlet, and lastly *aqua regii*.

GRANITE.

Mix black in about fifty times its quantity of water, and sprinkle equally over very fine, repeating it as it dries five or six times. Then, in like manner, sprinkle over with brown, and, after rubbing well, glaire lightly. Finally, sprinkle finely over with *aqua regii*.

TREE-MARBLES.

These marbles, which were first executed in Germany, from whence they passed into England, are formed by bending the boards in the middle, so that the water and colours flow from the back and foreedge to the centre, in the form of branches of trees. Those who have never seen the tree-marbles of Mr. Clarke, of London, can form but little idea of the beauty of which this style is susceptible. The name is also given to such as are made to imitate the grain of the wood.

WALNUT.

Formed by sprinkling black and brown only, as for the common marble.

CEDAR.

After sprinkling as for the walnut, and before perfectly dry, apply lightly a sponge presenting large holes dipped in orange upon various places on the cover, so as to form a description of clouds. Afterwards apply the fine red, with a similar sponge, nearly upon the same places, and when dry give the whole two or three coats of yellow, taking care that each penetrates evenly into the leather.

MAHOGANY.

The proceedings are nearly the same as for the walnut, the difference being merely in sprinkling the black more boldly, and, when perfectly dry, giving two or three uniform coats of red.

BOX.

In order to imitate the veins contained in box, the boards must be bent in five or six different places and in divers ways. After placing the book between the rods, throw on the water in small drops, and proceed as for the walnut. After being per-

22

fectly dry, throw water again in large drops, and sprinkle on small spots of blue, diluted equally with water; and, when again dry and rubbed well, apply the scarlet with a sponge as directed for the cedar. Finally, when dry, give two or three coats of orange, and the design is complete.

WAINSCOT.

Colour with strong brown, glaire, and place between the rods, with the boards flat. Throw on weak black in large spots, then brown in like manner, and, lastly, sprinkle boldly with vitriol-water.

VARIEGATED.

Marble as for the walnut, and then put on each board a circle, oval, or other figure, and apply weak black on the outer parts. When dry, give it a good coat of red, and, after throwing on spots of scarlet, take off the figures, and wash well the parts where the latter colour has been used. Finally, give the oval two coats of yellow, or other colour, with a camel's-hair brush.

MARBLING ON PAPER.

The sides of a half-bound book, which will be covered with paper, may be marbled to correspond with the effect produced on the leather by the action of the black and brown at the same time. This is performed by pasting firm white paper on the sides, and colouring with a mixture of four ounces of nut-galls and a small portion of powdered sal-ammo-niac boiled well together, which will take the black and brown nearly equal to leather.

SPRINKLES.

This is another ornament on the covers of books, capable of being much varied. A few of the most general use are given, premising that any of the colours arranged as for the marbles above, or sprinkled on the uniform colours, will be productive of a beautiful effect. The books must be paste-washed over, but not glaired.

NUTMEG.

Sprinkle very finely with black and then with brown. If wished to produce a finer effect, give a sprinkle of vitriol-water.

RING.

Put about a teaspoonful of vitriol to a cup of the black, and sprinkle coarsely over. If the ring is not sufficiently strong, add more vitriol.

TORTOISE-SHELL.

Wash the cover with yellow, and sprinkle very boldly with black. When dry, spot with a sponge, as before directed, with blue, red, and black, each colour being left to dry before the next is applied.

In concluding the description of the marbles and sprinkles, it may be remarked that, with a little taste, the workman might vary the designs to upwards of one hundred different patterns; also that each colour should be allowed to properly strike into the leather before another is used. Panes, or blank spaces, are formed by placing squares, &c. of pasteboard on the sides, which prevents the colours touching the leather when sprinkling. After the design is completed, the covers should be well rubbed with a woollen cloth or the ball of the hand, to remove the whole of the refuse of the colour, which will be found to corrode on the surface of the leather.

UNIFORM COLOURS.

Before proceeding to execute any of the colours, the books must be well and evenly paste-washed, and left till perfectly dry. It will also be necessary to observe that the black will become darker in all the subsequent operations of colouring, glairing, and polishing, so that attention must be paid not to use this liquid too strong.

LIGHT BROWN.

Wash the cover with vitriol-water till perfectly uniform in colour, and then with brown to the shade desired.

ANOTHER.

Mix a small quantity of annatto with the potash liquid, and use hot. This will produce a beautiful tint.

DARK BROWN.

Colour with weak black till a slate-shade is produced, and then apply the brown three or four times, as taste may dictate.

Others might be added, but the proceedings are the same, varying only the quantity of colour according to the shade. The *nut-brown liquid* will produce beautiful tints.

CORINTHIAN GRAPE.

The proceedings are the same as for the last colour, adding two or three coats of *fine red*.

22*

COMMON GRAPE.

Proceed as for the last, omitting the brown after the black.

BLUE.

After giving four or five coats of the chemical blue diluted with water, wash lightly with weakened aqua regii, which will take off the green reflection produced by the yellow tint of the leather.

GREEN.

Give three or four coats of the green liquid, extended in water according to the shade required. Any of the other colours noticed in the preparations may be thus executed.

OLIVE.

After giving a slate-colour, apply yellow, boiled with a small portion of blue, on the cover, rubbing it equally in while hot, to insure uniformity.

PEARL GRAY.

This colour must be executed carefully, so as to be perfectly uniform and without stains. Colour over with exceedingly weak black liquid, till a pale gray is produced. The weaker it is, the better will the workman succeed. Then pass over a light coat of fine red mixed in a large portion of water, so as to give a light red reflection scarcely distinguishable.

SLATE.

Use the black liquid a little stronger than for the last, and omit the red.

BLACK.

For common purposes, the black may be formed in the way adopted for other colours; but, in many instances, it is necessary to produce a colour having the appearance of japan, and which will require more labour and attention.

Wash the book over with brown till a dark shade is formed ; then, with a piece of woollen cloth, apply the black liquid mixed with japan, which will produce a beautiful black. This colour should have a good coat of vellum-size before glairing. Or it may be better to finish off with the varnish given in another part of the work.

Nutgalls, copperas, and gum-arabic, are used by many, and will be found to produce a good and bright colour.

GOLD MARBLES, LANDSCAPES, ETC.

These designs, if properly executed, are the most
beautiful that can be imagined. The labour and
care, however, requisite, must ever confine them to
superior bindings, for which a high price is given, to
indemnify the workman for the time required to
produce the proper effect. The imitation of the
gold marbles is not an easy task; but a knowledge
of the art of painting, and a clever management of
the brush, will enable the workman to imitate the
figure of the marble so true to nature as to be
scarcely distinguishable.

GOLD MARBLE.

This marble, which will not require the ability to
execute as those following it, is the invention of M.
Berthé, senior, bookbinder of Paris, and may be
executed on any kind of uniform substance. Take
a piece of cloth, exceeding the size of the volume,
and fold it equally; lay it, thus folded, evenly upon
a board, and then open the other half, and cover
the board; spread, upon the half towards the left,
gold leaf to the size of the cover, allowing such
portion as the roll intended to be worked on it may

take, which will be a saving of gold; then refold the cloth on the gold, and press the hand above, without moving the cloth, so as to divide the gold into a number of small pieces. The gold being thus prepared, moisten the side of the volume with glaire mixed with water in equal proportion, and place it on the cloth, pressing above firmly with the hand. Care being taken not to disarrange it, turn over the volume, cloth, and board, and take the latter off, replacing it with a sheet of paper, and rubbing smartly above, so as to attach the whole of the gold to the cover. After this the cloth must be removed, and the gold will be found equally fixed; to further insure which lay on a sheet of paper, and rub well with the palm of the hand.

To remove any gold that may appear on the part intended for the roll in gilding, wet the end of the thumb, form a sort of square with the fore-finger on the edge of the board to the size of the roll, and rub the surface of the cover, which will clear it .with facility before the glaire is dry.

LAPIS-LAZULI.

This marble is of clear blue, veined with gold, presenting an appearance of the utmost splendour. It is executed as follows :—

Place the volume between rods as for marbling, and with a sponge full of large holes, dipped in chemical blue mixed in six times its volume of water, make light spots, similar to clouds, at irregular distances; then put in a quarter part more blue, and make new clouds or spots a little darker. Repeat this operation six or seven times, each time adding more blue. All these coats will form stains in proper gradation, as in the natural marble; and to operate more properly, it would be better to have a model, either of the marble itself, or skilfully painted.

The veins of gold, which must not be laid on till the book is gilt, and just previous to polishing, are formed with gold in shell. The substance used to make it take and hold firmly on the cover of the book is prepared with white of egg and spirits of wine in equal proportion, and two parts of water, beating all well and leaving it to clear; then wet a small portion of gold-powder with the liquid, mixing it with the finger, and use it with a small camel's-hair pencil. Pass it on in different places, so as to imitate the model, according to the taste of the workman; when done, let it perfectly dry, and polish with the polisher scarcely warm.

It will be perceived that by the use of other

colours, or two or three together, many beautiful designs may be in like manner executed.

LANDSCAPES.

Many beautiful subjects may be formed on the sides of books by the workman skilled in painting; and, although coming more properly under the art of painting, and being objectionable on account of producing a mingling of the arts, so frequently exhibited upon volumes where the art of the bookbinder is superseded by that of the painter and jeweller, the young workman should understand at least the process by which they are produced. The volume is prepared by being pastewashed, so as to present a uniform fawn colour, the designs slightly traced, and afterwards coloured according to the pattern, the colours being mixed to the proper shade with water. The shades must be tried on pieces of refuse leather, as, being spirit-colours, when once laid on, no art can soften them down if too strong; and a peculiar lightness of touch will be necessary to produce effect. Portraits, &c. may also be executed in this manner, and many superb designs have at times been executed by the best binders of England and France. M. Didot, bookseller of Paris, presented a copy of the "*Hen riade,"* published by himself, to Louis XVIII., most elegantly ornamented in this style. It was executed by *M. Lunier Bellier*, bookbinder of Tours, and exhibited on one side a miniature portrait of Henry IV., and on the other a similar one of Louis XVIII., both perfect likenesses. The greatest difficulty consisted in the portraits, which were first imprinted on paper, very moist, and immediately applied to the cover, on which they were impressed with a flat roller. When perfectly dry, they were coloured with all the art of which the binder was capable, and the other ornamental paintings executed by hand. This proceeding requires great care in the execution, and will be applicable to any design where the binding will justify the expense.

TRANSFERRED LANDSCAPES.

The art of transferring, long practised in the ornamenting of fancy articles, was judged equally practicable for forming a superior embellishment for the sides of books. But the varnish necessary to be employed in the operation rendered the invention of no utility, from the action of the heated polisher turning it white or causing it to shell off. After several trials, this difficulty is believed to be overcome, by the employment of a very simple and common article in the office of the bookbinder,—viz.: *new glaire*, well beaten up. The proceeding is as follows :—Cut the print, intended to be transferred, close to the design on all sides. Let it steep in the glaire till it is well saturated with it. During this time glaire the book twice, letting it dry on each application. Take out the print, place it exactly in the centre of the side-cover, and, laying a piece of paper above, rub it sharply on the book, so that it may adhere very closely. Remove the upper paper, and with the finger rub off the paper gently until the printed design begins to appear, wetting the finger in *glaire* should the paper get too dry. The utmost attention will now be necessary, for the least carelessness in removing the paper that still remains may entirely destroy the design, and the whole of the previous labour be lost. The paper must be gently removed, piece by piece, till the design only appears on the leather while damp. When dry, a white appearance will be presented, arising from the small particles of paper adhering to the ink ; but these will be sufficiently hid on glairing the side previous to finishing. The extent and variety to which, at a small expense, these designs may be carried, with the finish and beauty

23

given to the sides of books, renders the subject
worthy of the attention of the ornamental workman
particularly; but he must possess perseverance and
carefulness in an eminent degree, to carry it to
perfection. After the gilding or other ornament is
executed, the side must be finished off in the usual
manner. A slight coat of the varnish described in
a subsequent part of the work will, in this case,
give a superior finish.

The following directions, and that of Mr.
Buchanan's, are taken from the circulars of the
Finishers' Friendly Association of London :—

"*Pictures on Calf.*—We have heard of a process
for transferring prints from the paper on which
they had been printed to the sides of books bound
in calf; and in these days, when *novelty* is so much
sought after, it might be worth some Friendly's
while to test its efficacy. The side must be washed
clean, and, while damp, the print is laid thereon,
when, after remaining some time in the arming-
press, it is said that a copy of the engraving will be
found on the calf.

"In sending one of these executed in colours by
him twenty years ago, a Friendly corrects an error
we committed, by terming *prints* PICTURES, and
writes, 'In preparing the calf, it is simply washed

with thin paste-water; when dry, a coat or two of
weak salts of tartar. When perfectly dry, you may
proceed with any subject; a very weak brown being
generally used for its outline. For all colours, I
use two cups of different strengths, with *quill*-pens
and brushes to each. The green is composed of
Scott's liquid blue and French berries. These are
bruised and simmered from half a pint to a quartern,
then caused to boil, and, while in that state, a
pinch of burnt alum should be added to set the
colour. The slate is weak copperas; red is obtained
from Brazil dust and vinegar, or Brazil chips boiled,
and solution of tin added. The books had generally
double bands—the lettering-pieces stained choco-
late, and the spaces between bands blacked, or the
colours " *moused*," morocco being too bright for the
stained calf. An octagon or square was coloured
brown, slate, or sprinkled, and in the centre a light
ground. Was the subject to my fancy, botanical
works with a group of plants on the sides, when
polished and pressed in japanned tins, had the
neatest appearance. Landscapes, animals, insects,
shells, &c. are all permanently fixed on the calf
by the above-named colours.' He concludes by
hoping 'the instructions are sufficiently plain to

induce some aspiring F. F.'s to practise this almost
forgotten branch of the art of finishing.'

"W. BUCHANAN."

ORNAMENTAL BLACK LINES.

Black lines in rays, or intersecting each other in
the form of diamonds or other devices, on the sides
of books, which present a good appearance if well
executed, are ruled with steel or swan pens, the
nibs being formed to the size required by the bold-
ness of the lines. The vinegar-black mixed with a
portion of gum-arabic, to neutralize a part of the
action of the acid and make it of a stronger consistency, will be found to answer best. Whatever the
pattern, it should be slightly traced with the folder,
and the design be afterwards marked with the pen,
kept steady by the aid of a ruler.

BLACKING THE SQUARES.

Unless coloured uniformly, the whole of the designs before described will not produce the best
effect if the squares remain plain or variously
tinted; it is, therefore, necessary to black the
edges and squares of the board, and the cap over
the head-band. This is done with a piece of any
firm soft substance on the edges, and with a sponge

within the volume, sufficiently below the part where the end-papers will cover. Finally, the covers should be well pastewashed and left to dry.

BANDS AND TITLE-PIECES.

Where the backs are flat it will be necessary to mark the place intended for the bands in gilding. For this purpose the binder should have patterns of the various forms and sizes cut out of thin board, a little longer and double the breadth of the volumes, so that they may be held firmly on the sides, while the bands are marked across the back through the apertures cut in the pattern. It is usual to give a double band at the bottom of the back, and therefore this must be allowed for in the pattern, which lengthened portion must be placed even with the edge of the boards at the tail of the volume, and the bands marked with the folder. By this plan the whole of the bands in sets of books will present a parallel line, and the bad effect produced by the inequalities arising from compassing the distances and trusting to the sight will be avoided. A great saving of time is also effected, as the patterns once made will serve for a very considerable period.

On the fancy colours and sprinkles it is usual to

23*

attach lettering-pieces of morocco. For this purpose the morocco, or roan if common work, is cut
lengthways of the grain, according to the space
between the bands, and the slip placed across the
back to measure the breadth, and then cut off. Then,
slightly damping on the flesh-side, it must be pared
as thin and equal as possible, and the edges sloped
evenly down, so as to bring it to the exact size
of the square it is to occupy. Should the back
require two pieces,—viz.: another for the volume or
contents,—it may be proper to vary the colour.
These title-pieces are pasted evenly on, a portion
of paste rubbed over them with the finger, and then
attached firmly and equally by rubbing down the
edges with the folder, when the paste must be well
washed off with a clean sponge. Where economy
is an object, the squares intended for the title may
be darkened with brown or black, which will show
the lettering very well.

INLAID ORNAMENTS.

To give some bindings in vellum, calf, or morocco
an additional degree of splendour, it is sometimes
required to execute ornaments on the covers of a
different colour; and, as this is an important manipulation, it will be necessary for the young workman

to understand it. Let the pattern be worked in blind upon the volume, taking care to have it well impressed. Pare morocco of the colour desired evenly and thin. While damp, place it upon that portion of the pattern to be inlaid, and press upon it with the fingers. The outline of the figure will appear through the morocco. Then lay it upon the paring-stone; and, with the same gouges with which the pattern has been executed, proceed to cut out the morocco. The gouges used for this kind of work should be made of steel.

The same directions will apply to fancy titles for flat backs.

After the pieces have been properly cut out, the workman will proceed to paste them evenly and adjust them in their place upon the volume.

When dry and prepared, the book will then be ready for gilding, and when covered with the gold ornament the joints of the leather will not be perceptible, if well executed. The gouges must be worked upon the edge of the morocco.

This kind of ornament is more frequently executed on calf than any other substance.

COLOURS.

In connection with inlaid ornament, we give a few hints to guide the workman in choice of colours. Much of the effect produced will result from the relations which the colours will bear to each other. A well-executed piece of work may be spoiled by the injudicious selection of colours. If the finisher be ignorant of the lessons which nature teaches in the distribution of colours, he cannot expect to please a connoisseur whose taste has been corrected and refined by a study of the harmonies of colours.

NUMERICAL PROPORTIONS OF HOMOGENEOUS COLOURS.

Yellow, 3.   *Red,* 5.   *Blue,* 8.

SECONDARIES.

3 Yellow 5 Red	Orange.	These are contrasting colours to the primaries with which they produce
5 Red 8 Blue	Purple.	harmony in opposition:—the orange with the blue, the purple with the
3 Yellow 8 Blue	Green.	yellow, and the green with the red.

TERTIARIES.

Purple Green	Olive.	The tertiaries stand in the same relation to the secondaries that the secon-
Green Orange	Citron.	daries do to the primaries:—olive to orange, citron to purple, and russet
Orange Purple	Russet.	to green.

Yellow is melodized by orange on one side and green on the other; blue by green and purple, and the red by purple and orange.

PASTING THE END-PAPERS, JOINTS, ETC.

The volume being laid upon the table or press, with the head towards the workman and the upper board open, the guard or false end-paper must be removed and all other substances cleared out of the joint with the folder. The paper to be pasted on the board is cut at each end, so as to show the same margin as on the fore-edge, and pasted evenly over. It is then carefully laid upon the board. The position being adjusted, a piece of white paper should be laid thereon, and the whole rubbed perfectly even with the flat of the hand. Then with the folder rub perfectly square on the joint. The volume, with the board open, may then be turned, and the other side done in the same way.

If it is intended to execute a gilt border or blind tooling in the interior of the cover, it will be important that no part of the end-paper covers it. To avoid this, a slip must be cut off at the head, tail, and on the fore-edge, proportionate to the extra breadth of the border over the square. Or, if morocco joints have been placed in the volume, the two corners of the portion left to be attached to the boards must be cut, to prevent their showing above the end-paper, which is to be pasted over and would disfigure the edge, taking care to leave as much leather as will cover perfectly such portion as is intended for the joint and square of the board, so that, when the paper is pasted on, it will not be perceived that the corners have been cut off. Pare the edge of the leather where the part is cut off on a small board or folder placed underneath; afterwards paste the joint on the edge of the board, attach it neatly with the thumb, finger, and folder, and, when dry, paste thereon the marbled or coloured paper cut to the proper size. For the best class of work the morocco joint is placed in the volume by the finisher after the book is covered.

If the ends are of silk, it will be necessary to leave the silk sufficiently large to turn the edges over a piece of paper that has been cut to the required size, and in order to preserve the gloss and richness of the silk it should not be pasted on the paper upon which it is placed, except where it is turned over the edge of the paper. The paper is then lightly glued over and adjusted upon the board. This method also prevents the silk from ravelling or presenting a jagged edge. In all cases, however, where the border is gilt or otherwise ornamented, below the level of the edges of the volume, the ends must not be pasted down till after that operation is completed, as the glaire and oil would be liable to stain, and present a bad effect.

For inferior bindings, where the end-papers are left plain, the last two leaves being merely pasted

STANDING-PRESS.

together, the ends will only require pasting, and attaching by placing the volume between boards, and screwing firmly in the standing-press, immediately after which it must be taken out and the boards opened, so as to make the joints free. Almost every class of work except velvet and Turkey morocco requires to be submitted to the action of the standing-press after the end-papers have been pasted down, and then allowed to become perfectly dry by leaving the boards open. Our illustration is taken from a standing-press manufactured by W. O. Hickok, Harrisburg, Pa.

In all the departments, but especially in finishing, cleanliness is of the utmost importance. It matters not how graceful may be the design, how perfectly the tools may be worked; all may be spoiled by a volume having a dirty appearance. Therefore, have every thing clean about you,—cups, sponges, and brushes. Let your size, pastewash, and glaire, be clean; your oil-cotton the same. Do not lay on the gold until the preparation is dry. After the working of your tools, be particular in cleaning off the gold, so that no portions or specks remain that should not, for they will have the appearance of dirt. In calf-work, especially, be careful of grease, or of any thing that will soil the leather. In summer-time great care must be taken to protect your work from the flies, particularly after your backs are worked off. The little pests will eat the glaire off in places, and give the book an unsightly appearance.

VARNISH,

AS USED IN BOOKBINDING.

The first, by the celebrated *Tingry*, is made in the following manner:—

Put into a vessel six ounces of mastic, in drops, three ounces of sandarac finely powdered, four ounces of coarsely-broken glass, separated from the dust by a sieve, and thirty-two ounces of spirits of wine, of about forty degrees. Place the vessel upon straw in another filled with cold water; put it on the fire and let it boil, stirring the substances together with a stick, to keep the resins from uniting. When the whole appears well mixed, put in three ounces of turpentine, and boil for another half-hour, when the whole must be taken off and stirred till the varnish and the water in which it is placed cools. Next day, filter it through a fine cotton, by which means it will acquire the greatest degree of limpidity, and well cork up in a bottle.

The other recipe is given by *Mons. F. Mairet*, of *Châtillon sur Seine*, and may be prepared similar to the above. The ingredients are, three pints of spirits of wine, of thirty-six to forty degrees, eight ounces of sandarac, two ounces of mastic in drops, eight ounces of shell-lac, and two ounces of Venice turpentine.

The varnish is first put on the back of the book with a camel's-hair brush as lightly as possible. When nearly dry, it is polished with a ball formed of fine white cotton, filled with wool, on which has been rubbed a small quantity of olive-oil, to make it glide freely; it must be rubbed at first lightly, and, as fast as the varnish dries and becomes warm, more sharply. The sides are in like manner polished one after the other.

Varnish is applied after the volume has been polished by the iron, in order to retain the brilliancy and preserve the volume from the bad effects produced by flies eating off the glaire. The manufactured article now in general use is applied by a soft sponge being lightly passed over the volumes after a small portion of varnish has been applied to the sponge.

STAMPING.

For gilding the sides and even backs of publishers' work, or in fact any other where a quantity of gilding is desired at little expense, the stamping-press is brought into requisition, and by means of tools cut for the purpose, called blocks or stamps, the design is impressed on the side. These stamps may be made of very small pieces, and, by having a number of them, the patterns produced may be almost indefinite. The stamps are affixed to an iron or brass plate, called a back or foundation-plate, upon which a piece of stout paper has been glued. Then let the workman mark upon the plate the exact size of the side to be stamped, marking it evenly with the compasses, so as to justify the stamps; then strike the centre, and draw lines upon the paper from the centre, so as to divide it into squares or to any given part, so as to afford freedom for selection in the starting-point of the design. For it must be manifest that if a workman starts all his patterns from the same point, notwithstanding he may have a variety of tools at his disposal, his patterns will exhibit a great deal of uniformity. Let the paper be glued equally over the surface, and proceed to form the pattern by arranging the stamps upon the plate so as to exhibit the design. A great deal of taste can be displayed in the formation of patterns for stamping; but, in consequence of the public generally desiring a mass of gilt gingerbread-work, this branch has been but little cultivated; the prevalent opinion among stampers being that it is no matter what is put upon the side so that it is well covered with gold. Publishers find those books that are the most tawdrily gilt are soonest disposed of; hence, every thing is sacrificed to a gaudy exterior. It is to be hoped that the art will be relieved from this degraded ornamentation. Stampers themselves can do something to purify and correct the public taste by avoiding the unmeaning collections confusedly huddled together, so often seen upon sides. Every remark in regard to style, design, and combination of tools in the hand-finisher's department applies with equal force to stamp-work; and, although the stamps used in the latter are not so plastic as those in hand-work, still great results will be achieved; for, notwithstanding the superiority of hand-work for artistic expression and permanence, press-work will always maintain a prominent position in the art, producing, as it does, striking results at a trifling expense. After the pattern is formed, take a little paste and touch the under side of each stamp, and place them in exact position. After this is done and the paste has become hard, lay the stamp or pattern thus formed upon the side of the volume, taking care to have the same margin on the front, back, and ends. Then place the board or side upon which the stamp is placed upon the platen or bed of the stamping-press, leaving the volume hanging down in front of the platen, which is then moved to the centre of the upper platen, so that the clamps will touch the plate on both edges at the same moment; then pull the lever so as to put a slight pressure upon the plate in order to keep both it and the side in their proper place; then adjust the guides to the fore-edge and head or left-hand side, and screw them fast; throw back the lever, take out the book; examine and correct any irregularity in the margin of the pattern by moving the guides. When perfectly square, place a soft pasteboard under the stamp, pull down the press, and apply heat. This will set the stamps or harden the paste and glue in a short time, so that they will not fall off in stamping — a great annoyance. Work for stamping does not require so much body or preparation as if it were to be gilt by hand. Morocco can be worked by merely being washed with urine; but it is safer to use a coat of size, or glaire and water

21*

mixed in proportions of one of the former to three
of the latter.   Grained sheep, or, as it is called,
imitation-morocco, requires more body to gild well.
After the books are ready for laying on, the gold-
leaf is cut upon the cushion to the required size, or,
if the volume be large and the stamp will cover its
superficial extent, the leaf may be lifted from the
gold-book by means of a block covered with wadding
or cotton lap and laid immediately upon the side.
After an oiled rag has been lightly passed over the
surface of the leather to cause the gold to adhere
until it is put under the press, examine the press
to see if sufficiently heated for the purpose.   A little
experience will soon determine the requisite amount
of heat as a general rule.   Leather-work does not
require as hot a tool for stamping as for hand-work,
while cloth or muslin-work requires a short, quick
stroke, and the press to be hotter than for leather.
In most binderies the stamping-press is heated by
introducing steam or gas through tubes perforated
for the purpose; though a few still use the heaters,
which, after being heated in a furnace, are placed
in the holes of the upper platen.   After the press
is properly heated, throw back the lever; take out
the pasteboard from under the stamp; regulate the
degree of pressure required for the stamp; then

place the side to be stamped upon the bed-plate, holding it firmly against the guides with the left hand, while with the right the lever is quickly drawn to the front. This straightens the toggles and causes a sharp impression of the stamp upon the leather; immediately throw back the lever; take out the side, and rub off with a rag the superfluous gold. Repeat the operation upon the other side, unless the stamp be of an upright design; it will then be necessary to turn the stamp in the press before operating upon the other side. Case-work or covers that are stamped before being put upon the books are done in the same manner, the backs

LETTERING AND GILDING PRESS, No. 1.

being also stamped before being glued on. The preceding cut of a stamping-press for gilding light

work, lettering, &c., is of the most approved construction, while for large, heavy work, either gilt or
stamped blind, (embossed, as it is erroneously called,)

EMBOSSING PRESS, No. 2.

and for cloth-work generally, the wheel-press is best
adapted. It can be worked either by hand or by
power. The fly-wheel can be kept revolving while
the workman is engaged in feeding the press. The
lever is used for light work. It will be perceived
that the upper platen of this press, to which the

Modernized Gothic

Modern Florinted Design

stamp is attached, is stationary, thereby giving great advantages in arranging pipes for heating by gas, and also for carrying off the smoke and unconsumed gas that would otherwise escape into the room. These presses are manufactured by I. Adams & Co., Boston.

A description of the various processes to produce by stamping the rich effects of inlaid work will be found under the head of Illuminated Binding and that of Inlaid Ornaments. For publishers' work it is a point of economy to have a steel-cutter that will cut out the pattern at one blow. For this kind of work, coloured German paper is used instead of leather for inlaying.

Thin boards are cut out with the aid of steel-cutters and the stamping-press, and affixed to the volumes; and, after they are covered, they are stamped in gold and blind with patterns corresponding with the figure of the cutter. This can only be applied where there are a large number of volumes, although single volumes may be cut out by hand at an increase of expense.

The modernized Gothic design (Plate IX.) is intended for a side-plate, to be worked either in gold or blank. The light floriated design (Plate X.) is calculated to be worked in gold, and is a good illustration of the prevailing treatment of the style for which it has been expressly designed. The pattern upon Plate XI. is intended for press-work, to be blank-stamped. The contrast of light and heavy work producing a fine effect, it is well adapted for a side-stamp, especially for cloth-work.

Plate XII. is a graceful design from a "Hint" of Mr. Leighton's. It is suited for a side-stamp, to be worked in gold; and with it closes our illustrations of design.

To obviate a difficulty that the young finisher will experience in his first attempts at designing, let him select a good quality of sized paper, cut it to the required size, then fold it carefully into four parts, and draw his pattern boldly upon one of the four corners with a lead-pencil. After that is done, slightly damp the opposite corner, fold the drawn portion so that it comes in contact with the damp surface, and rub it upon the back, so as to transfer the outlines of the drawing. When it appears with sufficient distinctness, trace it carefully over with the pencil, and repeat the process upon the other corners until the pattern is complete. This method insures accuracy and expedition. In working a pattern with gouges or with intersected lines, the same principle is applied, so as to reproduce the

Expressly for Cloth after Holbein's Style

From a hint of Leighton

pattern precisely alike at the four corners, and to save time. In this case the paper is folded, and one impression of the tool answers for both sides of the pattern.

Let the young finisher but feel a love for his art, make himself familiar with the best specimens, and determine to excel; and eventually his productions will be esteemed, his ability command the best situations, and he will be recognised as an artist.

CUTTING-MACHINES.

For cutting paper, pamphlets, and books " out of boards," a number of machines have been invented, and are used in many binderies, especially in those where large quantities of " cloth-work" are bound. They have been found to answer for this class of work very well. Some of them operate with sufficient nicety to cut books for case-work that are intended for gilt edges, when they are not to be scraped. For first-class work, cut " in boards," nothing has been discovered to supersede the old-fashioned mode of cutting with the plough and press.

PATENT PAPER AND BOOK TRIMMER.

The above cut of one of these machines, from the manufactory of I. Adams & Co., Boston, will serve to convey a general idea of its appearance; and the names of the makers are a sufficient guarantee of the mechanical perfection of its details.

TRANSLATION OF DATES.

Many old books have their dates printed in a manner which puzzles the finisher, should he be required to date any so printed, which are too thin to admit of its being done as on the title-page. The following key is here given, as it may be found useful in such cases:—c. 100; Iᴐ, or ᴅ, 500; cIᴐ or ᴍ, 1000; Iᴐᴐ, 5000; ccIᴐᴐ, 10,000; Iᴐᴐᴐ, 50,000, cccIᴐᴐᴐ, 100,000. Thus, cIᴐ, Iᴐ, ᴄʟxxxvɪɪɪ—1688. While on this subject, it may not be inappropriate to notice the dating of some books printed in France during the republic in that country. Thus, "An. xɪɪɪ."—1805, that being the thirteenth year of the republic, which commenced in 1792.

RESTORING THE BINDINGS OF OLD BOOKS.

Old bindings often look badly on account of the leather becoming dry and cracked, or the surface of the skin having been rubbed off in places. To obviate this, take a small quantity of paste and rub it carefully with the finger upon the

25

portions that require it; after it is dry, wash the
volume carefully over with a thin solution of glue
size. When dry, the volume may be varnished,
and afterwards rubbed over with a cloth in which
a few drops of sweet oil have been dropped.

SUPPLYING IMPERFECTIONS IN OLD BOOKS.

It often occurs that a valuable and rare work
has a leaf torn or missing. In order to supply it,
the first step will be to obtain the use of a perfect
copy as a model. Then procure paper of the
same colour as the leaf to be mended, and cut it
carefully to correspond with the torn portion.
After the piece has been neatly adjusted, tip
it and the leaf, very lightly, along the edges
with paste made of rice-flour; then place a piece
of tissue-paper on both sides of the leaf, and
smooth it carefully with the folder; then close
the volume and allow it to remain until perfectly
dry. Then proceed to remove the tissue-paper,
and it will be found that the portions that adhere
where the joining occurs will be strong enough
to secure the piece to the leaf of the book. The

letters may be then copied from the perfect copy and traced upon the inserted piece. The general appearance will depend upon the skill displayed in order to produce a successful imitation of the original.

HINTS

TO BOOK-COLLECTORS.

———

NEVER write your name upon the title-page of a book.

Have your books cut as large as possible, so as to preserve the integrity of the margin.

Do not adopt one style of binding for all your books.

Let the bindings upon your books be characteristic of the contents and of the value of the work.

Employ Turkey morocco for large works or for books that you have in constant use. It is the most durable material used in binding, except Levant morocco, which is very expensive.

English coloured calf makes a beautiful covering, and bears full gilt tooling better than morocco. The latter, if too richly charged, is apt to look tawdry.

292

Let the durability and neatness of your bindings be the primary requisites. Ornament judiciously and sparingly, rather than carelessly or gaudily.

Poetry and sermons are not to be treated alike, either in colour or degree of ornament to be employed.

The value of a library will be enhanced by the amount of knowledge and taste displayed in the bindings.

Russia leather is no protection against worms, and it speedily cracks along the joint.

Uncut books will command a higher price than those that are cropped.

To bind a book well, it should have ample time to dry after each process.

When you receive a volume from the binder, place it upon your shelf in such a manner that the adjoining volumes will press tightly against it and keep it closed; or, if you lay it upon your table, place other volumes upon it, to prevent the boards from warping, and do not, for some time, use it near the fire.

Upon opening a volume, do not grasp the leaves tightly in your hands. You might thereby break the back. If the book is too tight in the

25*

back, lay it upon a flat surface, and open it by taking a few sheets at a time, and lightly pressing upon the open leaves, going thus from the begining to the end, until the requisite freedom is obtained.

Use a paper-knife, or folder, to cut up the leaves of your uncut books, so that the edges will be smooth and even; otherwise the book will have to be cut down when it is bound.

Do not bind a newly-printed book. It is liable to set off in the pressing.

Never destroy an original binding upon an old volume if the binding be in tolerable condition. An old book should not be rebound, unless it is essential to its preservation; and then it should be, as far as possible, a restoration.

Carefully preserve old writings and autographs upon fly-leaves, unless they are trivial. It is an act of courtesy to the former owner of a book to place his book-plate on the end-board of the volume.

Any blank-leaves that occur in old volumes should not be removed. The bastard or half title should always be preserved.

Have all oblong plates placed in such a manner

that the inscription under them will read from the tail to the head of the volume.

Never bind a large map with a small volume. It is liable to tear away; and, in pressing the volume, it makes unseemly marks. Maps and plans should be affixed to blank leaves, so as to open clear of the volume, that the reader may have the plan and text to examine together

It is a false economy to bind up a number of volumes together, especially if they are of different sizes and upon different subjects.

Keep your books dry, but not too warm. Gas is injurious in a library, especially to the gilding upon the books.

Do not place books with uncut tops where the dust will fall upon them. It will penetrate between the leaves and mar the interior of the volumes.

Avoid placing books with clasps or carved sides upon the shelves. They will mark and scratch their neighbours

Never fold down corners, or wet your fingers, when reading or turning over the pages of a book.

Do not read a book at table. Crumbs are apt to penetrate into the back-fold of the leaves.

Books are not intended for card-racks or for receptacles of botanical specimens.

Never leave a book open, face downward, under
the pretext of keeping the place. If it remain
long in that condition, it will probably ever afterwards jump open at that place.

Never pull books out of the shelves by the headbands, or suffer them to stand long upon the
fore-edge.

Books should not be toasted before a fire or be
converted into cushions to sit upon.

Saturate a rag with camphor, and, when dry,
occasionally wipe the dust from your books with it,
and you will not be annoyed with book-worms.

Treat books gently; for "books are kind friends.
We benefit by their advice, and they exact no con-
fessions."

𝔗𝔢𝔠𝔥𝔫𝔦𝔠𝔞𝔩 𝔗𝔢𝔯𝔪𝔰

BOOKBINDING.

All-Along.—When a volume is sewed, and the thread passes from kettle-stitch to kettle-stitch, or from end to end in each sheet, it is said to be sewed all-along.

Asterisk.—A sign used by the printers at the bottom of the front page of the duplicate-leaves printed to supply the place of those cancelled.

Backing-Boards.—Are used for backing or forming the joint. They are made of very hard wood or faced with iron, and are thicker on the edge intended to form the groove than upon the edge that goes towards the fore-edge, so that the whole power of the laying-press may be directed towards the back.

Backing-Hammer.—The hammer used for backing
and rounding: it has a broad, flat face, similar
to a shoemaker's hammer.

Bands.—The twines whereon the sheets of a volume
are sewn.   When the book is sewed flexible
the bands appear upon the back.   When
the back is sawn so as to let in the twine,
the appearance of raised bands is produced
by glueing narrow strips of leather across
the back before the volume is covered.

Band-Driver.—A tool used in forwarding to correct irregularities in the bands of flexible
backs.

Bead.—The little roll formed by the knot of the
headband.

Bleed.—When a book is cut into the print it is said
to bleed.

Bevelled Boards.—Very heavy boards for the sides
champered around the edges

Blind-Tooled.—When the tools are impressed upon
the leather, without being gilt, they are said
to be blind or blank.

Boards.—Are of various kinds, such as pressing,
backing, cutting, burnishing, gilding, &c.
The pasteboards used for side-covers are
termed boards.   The boards used for cutting

books "out of boards" are called steamboat-boards. Tinned boards are used for finished work; while brass or iron-bound boards are used for pressing cloth-work.

Bodkin or Stabbing-Awl.—A strong point of iron or steel, fixed on a wooden handle, to form the holes in the boards required to lace in the bands. Used also for tracing the lines for cutting the fore-edge.

Bole.—A preparation used in gilding edges.

Bolt.—The fold in the head and fore-edge of the sheets. Also the small bar with a screw used to secure the knife to the plough.

Bosses.—Brass plates attached to the sides of volumes for their preservation.

Broke up.—When plates are turned over and folded at a short distance from the back-edge, before they are placed so as to enable them to turn easily in the volume, they are said to be broke up. The same process is sometimes applied to the entire volume.

Burnish.—The effect produced by the application of the burnisher to the edges.

Burnishers.—Are pieces of agate or bloodstone affixed to handles.

Cancels.—Leaves containing errors which are to be cut out and replaced with corrected pages.

Caps.—The leather covering of the headband. Applies also to the paper envelopes used to protect the edges while the volume is being covered and finished.

Case-Work.—Work in which the boards are covered and stamped. The volume is then glued upon the back and stuck into them.

Catch-Word.—A word met with in early-printed books at the bottom of the page, which word is the first on the following page. Now used to denote the first and last word in an encyclopædia or other book of reference.

Centre-Tools.—Are single, upright, or independent tools used for the middle of the panels by the finisher.

Clearing Out. — Removing the waste-paper and paring away any superfluous leather upon the inside, preparatory to pasting down the lining-paper.

Collating.—Examining the signatures, after the volume is gathered, to ascertain if they be correct and follow in numerical order.

Corners. — The triangular brass tools used in

finishing backs and sides. The gilt ornaments used on velvet books. Also, the
leather pasted on the corners of half-bound
books.

Creaser.--The tool used in marking each side of the
bands, generally made of steel.

Cropped.—When a book has been cut down too
much it is said to be cropped.

Dentelle.—A fine tooled border resembling lace-
work.

Edge-Rolled.—When the edges of the boards are
rolled. It may be either in gold or blind.

Embossed.—When a plate is stamped upon the
cover so as to present a raised figure or
design, it is said to be embossed. Some
inappropriately term this kind of work Arabesque.

End-Papers.—The paper placed at each end of the
volume, a portion of which is removed when
the lining-paper is pasted down upon the
boards. Also called Waste-Papers.

Fillet.—The cylindrical ornament used in finishing
upon which simple lines are engraved.

26

Finishing.—Is that department that receives the volumes after they are put in leather, and ornaments them as required. One who works at this branch is termed a finisher.

Finishers' Press.—Is the same as a laying-press, only much smaller.

Flexible.—When a book is sewn on raised bands and the thread is passed entirely round each band.

Folder.—This is a flat piece of bone or ivory used in folding the sheets and in many other manipulations. Also applied to a female engaged in folding sheets.

Fore-Edge.—The front edge of the book.

Foundation-Plate.—A plate of iron or brass upon which side-stamps are affixed.

Forwarding.—Is that branch that takes the books after they are sewed and advances them until they are put in leather ready for the finisher. One who works at this branch is termed a forwarder.

Full-Bound.—When the sides of a volume are entirely covered with leather, it is said to be full-bound.

Gathering.—The process of arranging the sheets according to the signatures.

Gauge.—Used in forwarding to take the correct size of the volume and to mark it upon the boards for squaring.

Gilt.—Is applied to both the edges and to the ornaments in finishing.

Glaire.—The whites of eggs.

Grater.—An iron instrument used by the forwarder for rubbing the backs after they are paste-washed.

Gouge.—A tool used in finishing, the face of which is a line forming the segment of a circle.

Guards.—Strips of paper inserted in the backs of books intended for the insertion of plates, to prevent the book being uneven when filled; also the strips upon which plates are mounted.

Guides.—The groove in which the plough moves upon the face of the cutting-press.

Half-Bound. — When a volume is covered with leather upon the back and corners, and the sides are covered with paper or cloth.

Hand-Letters.—Letters cut and affixed to handles,

and adjusted singly upon the volume when lettering it.

Head and Tail.—The top and bottom of a book.

Headband.—The silk or cotton ornament worked at the ends so as to make the back even with the squares.

Imperfections.—Sheets rejected on account of being in some respect imperfect, and for which others are required to make the work complete.

In Boards.—When a volume is cut after the pasteboards are affixed to form the sides, it is said to be cut in boards. The term is also applied to a style of binding in which the boards are merely covered with paper.

Inset.—The pages cut off in folding and placed in the middle of the sheet.

Inside Tins.—So called from being placed inside of the boards when the volume is put in the standing-press.

Joints.—The projections formed in backing to admit the boards; applied also to the inside when the volume is covered.

Justification. — The observance that the pages of a volume agree and are parallel throughout, so as to insure a straight and equal margin.

Kettle-Stitch.—The stitch which the sewer makes at the head and tail of a book; said to be a corruption of chain-stitch.

Keys.—The little instruments used to secure the bands to the sewing-press.

Knocking-Down Iron, so called from having the slips, when laced in, pounded down upon it, so that they will not show when the book is covered.

Laced In.—When the boards are affixed to the volume by means of the bands being passed through holes made in the boards, they are said to be laced in.

Lettering-Block.—A piece of wood, the upper surface being rounded, upon which side-labels are lettered.

Lettering-Box.—The box in which the type are screwed up preparatory to lettering.

Lining-Paper.—The coloured or marbled paper at each end of the volume.

26*

Marbler.—The workman who marbles the edges of
books, &c.

Mitred.—When the lines in finishing intersect each
other at right angles and are continued without overrunning each other, they are said to
be mitred.

Out of Boards.—When a volume is cut before the
boards are affixed, it is said to be done out
of boards.

Overcasting.—An operation in sewing, when the
work consists of single leaves or plates.

Pallet.—Name given to the tools used in gilding
upon the bands, sometimes applied to the
lettering-box.

Panel.—The space between bands; also applied to
bevelled and sunk sides.

Papering Up.—Covering the edges after they are
gilt, so as to protect them while the volume
is being covered and finished.

Paring.—Reducing the edges of the leather by
forming a gradual slope.

Pastewash.—A thin dilution of paste in water.

Pencil.—A small brush of camel's hair.

Pieced.—When the space between bands, upon

which the lettering is placed, has a piece of leather upon it different from the back, it is said to be pieced or titled.

Plough.—The instrument used in cutting the edges of books and pasteboards.

Points.—Holes made in the sheets by the printer; they serve as guides in folding.

Polisher.—A steel implement used in finishing.

Press.—There are various kinds of presses,—viz.: laying or cutting, standing, stamping, embossing, gilding, and finishing.

Rake.—An instrument used in forwarding, to harden the backs while being pastewashed in the standing-press.

Rasped.—The sharp edge taken off the boards.

Register.—The ribbon placed in a volume for a marker; also a list of signatures, attached to the end of early-printed works, for the use of the binder.

Rolls.—The cylindrical ornaments used in finishing.

Run Up.—When the back has a fillet run from head to tail without being mitred at each band, it is said to be run up.

Runner. — The front board used in cutting edges, &c.

Sewer.—The person who sews the sheets together on the sewing-press—generally a female.

Set-Off.—Designates the transfer of the ink to the opposite page.

Setting the Head.—Is covering the headband neatly with the leather, so as to form a kind of cap.

Shaving-Tub.—The paper cut from the edges of a volume are called shavings. The receptacle into which they fall while the forwarder is cutting the edges is termed the shaving-tub.

Signature.—The letter or figure under the footline of the first page of each sheet to indicate the order of arrangement in the volume; sometimes applied to the sheet itself.

Size.—A preparation used in finishing and gilding, generally made from vellum.

Slips.—The pieces of twine that project beyond the volume after it is sewn.

Squares.—The portions of the board that project over the edges.

Stabbing.—The operation of piercing the boards with a bodkin for the slips to pass through; also the piercing of pamphlets for the purpose of stitching.

Stamps.—The brass tools used in finishing to impress a figure upon the leather ; they are distinguished by hand-stamps and stamps for the press.

Start.—When any of the leaves are not properly secured in the back, upon opening the volume they will project beyond the others, and are said to start.

Steamboating.—Cutting books out of boards, a number being cut at the same time.

Stitching.—The operation of passing the thread through a pamphlet for the purpose of securing the sheets together.

Stops.—Are small circular tools, adapted to stop a fillet when it intersects at right angles, to save the time used in mitreing.

Title.—The space between bands, upon which the lettering is placed.

Tools.—Applied particularly to the hand-stamps and tools used in finishing.

Trindle.—A strip of thin wood or iron.

Turning Up.—The process of cutting the fore-edges in such a manner as to throw the round out of the back until the edge is cut.

Tying Up.—The tying of a volume after the cover has been drawn on, so as to make the leather

adhere to the sides of the bands; also for
setting the head.

Whipping.—The process of overseaming plates.

Witness.—When a volume is cut so as to show that
it has not been cut as small as some of the
leaves, their uncut edges prove this, and
are called witness and sometimes proof.

Wrinkle.—The uneven surfaces in a volume, caused
by not being properly pressed or by dampness, also caused by improper backing.

INDEX.

311

Dawson, 20.
Derome, 18, 19, 67.
De Seuil, 18, 19.
Design, 186.
Designing, 286.
De Thou, bindings of, 19.
Dibdin, his account of the library of Corvinus, 14.
—— of Roger Payne, 26, 191, 195.
Diptych, description of, 11.
Drag Spanish marble, 114.
Drop ivory black, 91.
Drop lake, 86.
Dutch marble, 120.
Duru, 31, 32.
Dutch pink, 90.

Edges, colouring and sprinkling, 74.
—— colours for, 74–79.
—— blue, 78.
—— yellow, 78.
—— green, 78.
—— orange, 78.
—— red, 78.
—— purple, 79.
—— brown, 79.
—— black, 136.
—— rice marbled, 80.
—— white spotted, 80.
—— fancy marbled, 81.
—— gold sprinkle, 81.
—— marbled, 82, 125.
—— burnishing, 125, 129.
—— gilt, 130.
—— antique, 134.

Edges, gold upon marble, 135.
—— black, 136.
Edge-gilding, 130.
———— antique, 134.
———— on marble, 135.
———— on landscapes, 135.
Eighteenmo, 36.
Elizabethan, 184.
End-papers, 59, 60, 273.
Etruscan, 180.
Eyton, J. W. King, binding belonging to, 28, 29.

Fair agate marble, on leather, 249.
Falkner, 28.
Fancy titles, 221, 271.
Fawn, colour for leather, 244.
Finishing, blank-work, 168.
Finisher's standing press, 275.
Flea-seed, 94.
Flexible, mode of sewing, 53.
—— marking off, 54, 55.
Folding, 35.
—— blank-work, 157.
Folio, 36.
Font Hill, 150, 205.
Forwarding, job-work, mode of operation, 59.
—— making end-papers, 60.
—— putting in joints, 61.
—— glueing up, rounding, 62.
—— backing, 63, 64.
—— cutting, 65, 70.
—— making boards, 65.
—— squaring, 66.
—— lacing in, 68.

27

Sewing-bench, 49, 50.
Shell marble, 100, 103, 104.
Sheriffs of Shropshire, 28.
Sheet-work, 35.
Silk lining, 274.
Sixteenmo, 36.
Sizing the paper, 127.
Slate, uniform colour for lea-
ther, 259.
Smasher, substitute for beat-
ing, 44.
—— mode of operation; amount
of pressure; advantage
of, 45.
Spanish marble, 110.
————— olive, 111.
————— blue, 112.
————— brown, 112.
————— fancy, 113.
————— drag, 114.
Spring-back, blank-work, 161.
Sprinkles, 255, 256.
Sprinkling, mode of, 75, **76.**
—— colours for, 74.
—— rice-marble, 80.
—— white spot, 80.
—— gold sprinkle, 81.
Staggemier, 20.
Stamping, 279.
Steamboating, 172.
Stabbing, 68.
Steel gouges, 271.
Stone marble, on leather, 248.
Sunk boards, 285.
Supplying imperfections in old
books, 290

Table-shears, 175.
Taste, 186.
Technical terms, 297–310.
Tertiary colours, 272.
Thirty-twomo, 36.
Thouvenin, bindings of, 30.
Titles, 269.
—— fancy, 271.
Tortoise-shell sprinkle on lea
ther, 256.
To dissolve gold, 237.
Transfers, 264, 266.
Transferring designs, 286.
Translation of dates, 289.
Trautz et Bauzonnet, 31, 32,
142.
Tree-marbled calf, 28, 252.
Troughs for marbling, 100.
Turning up, 72.
Twelvemo, 36, 37.
Twenty-fourmo, 36.
Tying up, 146.

Ultramarine, 89.
Umber, 91.
Uncut books, 151.
Uniform colours on leather,
256–259.

Variegated marble, on lea-
ther, 254.
Varnish, 277.
Vegetable black, 91.
Vermilion, 87.
Violet for leather, 243.
Vitriol-water for marbling lea-
ther, 240.

THE END.

STEREOTYPED BY L. JOHNSON AND CO.
PHILADELPHIA.

CATALOGUE

OF

PRACTICAL AND SCIENTIFIC BOOKS,

PUBLISHED BY

HENRY CAREY BAIRD & CO.,

Industrial Publishers and Booksellers,

NO. 810 WALNUT STREET,

PHILADELPHIA.

☞ Any of the Books comprised in this Catalogue will be sent by mail, free of postage, at the publication price.

☞ A Descriptive Catalogue, 96 pages, 8vo., will be sent, free of postage, to any one who will furnish the publisher with his address.

ARLOT.—A Complete Guide for Coach Painters.
Translated from the French of M. ARLOT, Coach Painter; for eleven years Foreman of Painting to M. Eherler, Coach Maker, Paris. By A. A. FESQUET, Chemist and Engineer. To which is added an Appendix, containing Information respecting the Materials and the Practice of Coach and Car Painting and Varnishing in the United States and Great Britain. 12mo. $1.25

ARMENGAUD, AMOROUX, and JOHNSON.—The Practical Draughtsman's Book of Industrial Design, and Machinist's and Engineer's Drawing Companion:
Forming a Complete Course of Mechanical Engineering and Architectural Drawing. From the French of M. Armengaud the elder, Prof. of Design in the Conservatoire of Arts and Industry, Paris, and MM. Armengaud the younger, and Amoroux, Civil Engineers. Rewritten and arranged with additional matter and plates, selections from and examples of the most useful and generally employed mechanism of the day. By WILLIAM JOHNSON, Assoc. Inst. C. E., Editor of "The Practical Mechanic's Journal." Illustrated by 50 folio steel plates, and 50 wood-cuts. A new edition, 4to. $10.00

1

ARROWSMITH.—Paper-Hanger's Companion:
A Treatise in which the Practical Operations of the Trade are Systematically laid down : with Copious Directions Preparatory to Papering ; Preventives against the Effect of Damp on Walls ; the Various Cements and Pastes Adapted to the Several Purposes of the Trade ; Observations and Directions for the Panelling and Ornamenting of Rooms, etc. By JAMES ARROWSMITH, Author of "Analysis of Drapery," etc. 12mo., cloth. $1.25

ASHTON.—The Theory and Practice of the Art of Designing Fancy Cotton and Woollen Cloths from Sample:
Giving full Instructions for Reducing Drafts, as well as the Methods of Spooling and Making out Harness for Cross Drafts, and Finding any Required Reed, with Calculations and Tables of Yarn. By FREDERICK T. ASHTON, Designer, West Pittsfield, Mass. With 52 Illustrations. One volume, 4to. $10.00

BAIRD.—Letters on the Crisis, the Currency and the Credit System.
By HENRY CAREY BAIRD. Pamphlet.   05

BAIRD.—Protection of Home Labor and Home Productions necessary to the Prosperity of the American Farmer.
By HENRY CAREY BAIRD. 8vo., paper.   10

BAIRD.—Some of the Fallacies of British Free-Trade Revenue Reform.
Two Letters to Arthur Latham Perry, Professor of History and Political Economy in Williams College. By HENRY CAREY BAIRD. Pamphlet.   05

BAIRD.—The Rights of American Producers, and the Wrongs of British Free-Trade Revenue Reform.
By HENRY CAREY BAIRD. Pamphlet.   05

BAIRD.—Standard Wages Computing Tables:
An Improvement in all former Methods of Computation, so arranged that wages for days, hours, or fractions of hours, at a specified rate per day or hour, may be ascertained at a glance. By T. SPANGLER BAIRD. Oblong folio. $5.00

BAIRD.—The American Cotton Spinner, and Manager's and Carder's Guide:
A Practical Treatise on Cotton Spinning ; giving the Dimensions and Speed of Machinery, Draught and Twist Calculations, etc. ; with notices of recent Improvements : together with Rules and Examples for making changes in the sizes and numbers of Roving and Yarn. Compiled from the papers of the late ROBERT H. BAIRD. 12mo. $1.50

BAKER.—Long-Span Railway Bridges :
Comprising Investigations of the Comparative Theoretical and Practical Advantages of the various Adopted or Proposed Type Systems of Construction; with numerous Formulæ and Tables. By B. BAKER. 12mo. $2.00

BAUERMAN.—A Treatise on the Metallurgy of Iron :
Containing Outlines of the History of Iron Manufacture, Methods of Assay, and Analysis of Iron Ores, Processes of Manufacture of Iron and Steel, etc., etc. By H. BAUERMAN, F. G. S., Associate of the Royal School of Mines. First American Edition, Revised and Enlarged. With an Appendix on the Martin Process for Making Steel, from the Report of ABRAM S. HEWITT, U. S. Commissioner to the Universal Exposition at Paris, 1867. Illustrated. 12mo. . $2.00

BEANS.—A Treatise on Railway Curves and the Location of Railways.
By E. W. BEANS, C. E. Illustrated. 12mo. Tucks. . . $1.50

BELL.—Carpentry Made Easy :
Or, The Science and Art of Framing on a New and Improved System. With Specific Instructions for Building Balloon Frames, Barn Frames, Mill Frames, Warehouses, Church Spires, etc. Comprising also a System of Bridge Building, with Bills, Estimates of Cost, and valuable Tables. Illustrated by 38 plates, comprising nearly 200 figures. By WILLIAM E. BELL, Architect and Practical Builder. 8vo. . $5.00

BELL.—Chemical Phenomena of Iron Smelting.
An Experimental and Practical Examination of the Circumstances which determine the Capacity of the Blast Furnace, the Temperature of the Air, and the proper Condition of the Materials to be operated upon. By I. LOWTHIAN BELL. Illustrated. 8vo. . . $6.00

BEMROSE.—Manual of Wood Carving :
With Practical Illustrations for Learners of the Art, and Original and Selected Designs. By WILLIAM BEMROSE, Jr. With an Introduction by LLEWELLYN JEWITT, F. S. A., etc. With 128 Illustrations. 4to., cloth. $3.00

BICKNELL.—Village Builder, and Supplement :
Elevations and Plans for Cottages, Villas, Suburban Residences, Farm Houses, Stables and Carriage Houses, Store Fronts, School Houses, Churches, Court Houses, and a model Jail; also, Exterior and Interior details for Public and Private Buildings, with approved Forms of Contracts and Specifications, including Prices of Building Materials and Labor at Boston, Mass., and St. Louis, Mo. Containing 75 plates drawn to scale; showing the style and cost of building in different sections of the country, being an original work comprising the designs of twenty leading architects, representing the New England, Middle, Western, and Southwestern States. 4to. . $12.00

BLENKARN.—Practical Specifications of Works executed in Architecture, Civil and Mechanical Engineering, and in Road Making and Sewering:
To which are added a series of practically useful Agreements and Reports. By JOHN BLENKARN. Illustrated by 15 large folding plates.
8vo. $9.00

BLINN.—A Practical Workshop Companion for Tin, Sheet-Iron, and Copperplate Workers :
Containing Rules for describing various kinds of Patterns used by Tin, Sheet-Iron, and Copper-plate Workers; Practical Geometry; Mensuration of Surfaces and Solids; Tables of the Weights of Metals, Lead Pipe, etc.; Tables of Areas and Circumferences of Circles; Japan, Varnishes, Lackers, Cements, Compositions, etc., etc. By LEROY J. BLINN, Master Mechanic. With over 100 Illustrations.
12mo. $2.50

BOOTH.—Marble Worker's Manual :
Containing Practical Information respecting Marbles in general, their Cutting, Working, and Polishing; Veneering of Marble; Mosaics; Composition and Use of Artificial Marble, Stuccos, Cements, Receipts, Secrets, etc., etc. Translated from the French by M. L. BOOTH. With an Appendix concerning American Marbles. 12mo., cloth. $1.50

BOOTH AND MORFIT.—The Encyclopedia of Chemistry, Practical and Theoretical :
Embracing its application to the Arts, Metallurgy, Mineralogy, Geology, Medicine, and Pharmacy. By JAMES C. BOOTH, Melter and Refiner in the United States Mint, Professor of Applied Chemistry in the Franklin Institute, etc., assisted by CAMPBELL MORFIT, author of "Chemical Manipulations," etc. Seventh edition. Royal 8vo., 978 pages, with numerous wood-cuts and other illustrations.   . $5.00

BOX.—A Practical Treatise on Heat :
As applied to the Useful Arts ; for the Use of Engineers, Architects, etc. By THOMAS BOX, author of " Practical Hydraulics." Illustrated by 14 plates containing 114 figures. 12mo. $4.25

BOX.—Practical Hydraulics :
A Series of Rules and Tables for the use of Engineers, etc. By THOMAS BOX. 12mo. $2.50

BROWN.—Five Hundred and Seven Mechanical Movements :
Embracing all those which are most important in Dynamics, Hydraulics, Hydrostatics, Pneumatics, Steam Engines, Mill and other Gearing, Presses, Horology, and Miscellaneous Machinery ; and including many movements never before published, and several of which have only recently come into use. By HENRY T. BROWN, Editor of the "American Artisan." In one volume, 12mo.   .   .   . $1.00

BUCKMASTER.—The Elements of Mechanical Physics :
By J. C. BUCKMASTER, late Student in the Government School of Mines; Certified Teacher of Science by the Department of Science and Art; Examiner in Chemistry and Physics in the Royal College of Preceptors; and late Lecturer in Chemistry and Physics of the Royal Polytechnic Institute. Illustrated with numerous engravings. In one volume, 12mo. $1.50

BULLOCK.—The American Cottage Builder :
A Series of Designs, Plans, and Specifications, from $200 to $20,000, for Homes for the People; together with Warming, Ventilation, Drainage, Painting, and Landscape Gardening. By JOHN BULLOCK, Architect, Civil Engineer, Mechanician, and Editor of " The Rudiments of Architecture and Building," etc., etc. Illustrated by 75 engravings. In one volume, 8vo. $3.50

BULLOCK.—The Rudiments of Architecture and Building :
For the use of Architects, Builders, Draughtsmen, Machinists, Engineers, and Mechanics. Edited by JOHN BULLOCK, author of " The American Cottage Builder." Illustrated by 250 engravings. In one volume, 8vo. $3.50

BURGH.—Practical Illustrations of Land and Marine Engines :
Showing in detail the Modern Improvements of High and Low Pressure, Surface Condensation, and Super-heating, together with Land and Marine Boilers. By N. P. BURGH, Engineer. Illustrated by 20 plates, double elephant folio, with text. . . . $21.00

BURGH.—Practical Rules for the Proportions of Modern Engines and Boilers for Land and Marine Purposes.
By N. P. BURGH, Engineer. 12mo. $1.50

BURGH.—The Slide-Valve Practically Considered.
By N. P. BURGH, Engineer. Completely illustrated. 12mo. $2.00

BYLES.—Sophisms of Free Trade and Popular Political Economy Examined.
By a BARRISTER (Sir JOHN BARNARD BYLES, Judge of Common Pleas). First American from the Ninth English Edition, as published by the Manchester Reciprocity Association. In one volume, 12mo. Paper, 75 cts. Cloth $1.25

BYRN.—The Complete Practical Brewer :
Or Plain, Accurate, and Thorough Instructions in the Art of Brewing Beer, Ale, Porter, including the Process of making Bavarian Beer, all the Small Beers, such as Root-beer, Ginger-pop, Sarsaparilla-beer, Mead, Spruce Beer, etc., etc. Adapted to the use of Public Brewers and Private Families. By M. LA FAYETTE BYRN, M.D. With illustrations. 12mo. $1.25

BYRN.—The Complete Practical Distiller:

Comprising the most perfect and exact Theoretical and Practical Description of the Art of Distillation and Rectification; including all of the most recent improvements in distilling apparatus; instructions for preparing spirits from the numerous vegetables, fruits, etc.; directions for the distillation and preparation of all kinds of brandies and other spirits, spirituous and other compounds, etc., etc. By M. LA FAYETTE BYRN, M. D. Eighth Edition. To which are added, Practical Directions for Distilling, from the French of Th. Fling, Brewer and Distiller. 12mo. $1.50

BYRNE.—Handbook for the Artisan, Mechanic, and Engineer:

Comprising the Grinding and Sharpening of Cutting Tools, Abrasive Processes, Lapidary Work, Gem and Glass Engraving, Varnishing and Lackering, Apparatus, Materials and Processes for Grinding and Polishing, etc. By OLIVER BYRNE. Illustrated by 185 wood engravings. In one volume, 8vo. $5.00

BYRNE.—Pocket Book for Railroad and Civil Engineers:

Containing New, Exact, and Concise Methods for Laying out Railroad Curves, Switches, Frog Angles, and Crossings; the Staking out of work; Levelling; the Calculation of Cuttings; Embankments; Earth-work, etc. By OLIVER BYRNE. 18mo., full bound, pocketbook form $1.75

BYRNE.—The Practical Model Calculator:

For the Engineer, Mechanic, Manufacturer of Engine Work, Naval Architect, Miner, and Millwright. By OLIVER BYRNE. 1 volume, 8vo., nearly 600 pages $4.50

·BYRNE.—The Practical Metal-Worker's Assistant:

Comprising Metallurgic Chemistry; the Arts of Working all Metals and Alloys; Forging of Iron and Steel; Hardening and Tempering; Melting and Mixing; Casting and Founding; Works in Sheet Metal; The Processes Dependent on the Ductility of the Metals; Soldering; and the most Improved Processes and Tools employed by Metal-Workers. With the Application of the Art of Electro-Metallurgy to Manufacturing Processes; collected from Original Sources, and from the Works of Holtzapffel, Bergeron, Leupold, Plumier, Napier, Scoffern, Clay, Fairbairn, and others. By OLIVER BYRNE. A new, revised, and improved edition, to which is added An Appendix, containing THE MANUFACTURE OF RUSSIAN SHEET-IRON. By JOHN PERCY, M. D., F.R.S. THE MANUFACTURE OF MALLEABLE IRON CASTINGS, and IMPROVEMENTS IN BESSEMER STEEL. By A. A. FESQUET, Chemist and Engineer. With over 600 Engravings, illustrating every Branch of the Subject. 8vo. $7.00

Cabinet Maker's Album of Furniture:

Comprising a Collection of Designs for Furniture. Illustrated by 48 Large and Beautifully Engraved Plates. In one vol., oblong $5.00

CALLINGHAM.—Sign Writing and Glass Embossing:

A Complete Practical Illustrated Manual of the Art. By JAMES CALLINGHAM. In one volume, 12mo. $1.50

CAMPIN.—A Practical Treatise on Mechanical Engineering:

Comprising Metallurgy, Moulding, Casting, Forging, Tools, Workshop Machinery, Mechanical Manipulation, Manufacture of Steam-engines, etc., etc. With an Appendix on the Analysis of Iron and Iron Ores. By FRANCIS CAMPIN, C. E. To which are added, Observations on the Construction of Steam Boilers, and Remarks upon Furnaces used for Smoke Prevention; with a Chapter on Explosions. By R. Armstrong, C. E., and John Bourne. Rules for Calculating the Change Wheels for Screws on a Turning Lathe, and for a Wheel-cutting Machine. By J. LA NICCA. Management of Steel, Including Forging, Hardening, Tempering, Annealing, Shrinking, and Expansion. And the Case-hardening of Iron. By G. EDE. 8vo. Illustrated with 29 plates and 100 wood engravings . . . $6.00

CAMPIN.—The Practice of Hand-Turning in Wood, Ivory, Shell, etc.:

With Instructions for Turning such works in Metal as may be required in the Practice of Turning Wood, Ivory, etc. Also, an Appendix on Ornamental Turning. By FRANCIS CAMPIN; with Numerous Illustrations. 12mo., cloth $3.00

CAREY.—The Works of Henry C. Carey:

FINANCIAL CRISES, their Causes and Effects. 8vo. paper . 25

HARMONY OF INTERESTS: Agricultural, Manufacturing, and Commercial. 8vo., cloth $1.50

MANUAL OF SOCIAL SCIENCE. Condensed from Carey's "Principles of Social Science." By KATE McKEAN. 1 vol. 12mo. $2.25

MISCELLANEOUS WORKS: comprising "Harmony of Interests," "Money," "Letters to the President," "Financial Crises," "The Way to Outdo England Without Fighting Her," "Resources of the Union," "The Public Debt," "Contraction or Expansion?" "Review of the Decade 1857–'67," "Reconstruction," etc., etc. Two vols., 8vo., cloth $10.00

PAST, PRESENT, AND FUTURE. 8vo. $2.50

PRINCIPLES OF SOCIAL SCIENCE. 3 vols., 8vo., cloth $10.00

THE SLAVE-TRADE, DOMESTIC AND FOREIGN; Why it Exists, and How it may be Extinguished (1853). 8vo., cloth . $2.00

LETTERS ON INTERNATIONAL COPYRIGHT (1867) . 50

THE UNITY OF LAW: As Exhibited in the Relations of Physical, Social, Mental, and Moral Science (1872). In one volume, 8vo., pp. xxiii., 433. Cloth $3.50

CHAPMAN.—A Treatise on Ropemaking:

As Practised in private and public Rope yards, with a Description of the Manufacture, Rules, Tables of Weights, etc., adapted to the Trades, Shipping, Mining, Railways, Builders, etc. By ROBERT CHAPMAN. 24mo. $1.50

COLBURN.—The Locomotive Engine:
Including a Description of its Structure, Rules for Estimating its Capabilities, and Practical Observations on its Construction and Management. By ZERAH COLBURN. Illustrated. A new edition. 12mo. $1.25

CRAIK.—The Practical American Millwright and Miller.
By DAVID CRAIK, Millwright. Illustrated by numerous wood engravings, and two folding plates. 8vo. $5.00

DE GRAFF.—The Geometrical Stair Builders' Guide:
Being a Plain Practical System of Hand-Railing, embracing all its necessary Details, and Geometrically Illustrated by 22 Steel Engravings; together with the use of the most approved principles of Practical Geometry. By SIMON DE GRAFF, Architect. 4to. . $5.00

DE KONINCK.—DIETZ.—A Practical Manual of Chemical Analysis and Assaying:
As applied to the Manufacture of Iron from its Ores, and to Cast Iron, Wrought Iron, and Steel, as found in Commerce. By L. L. DE KONINCK, Dr. Sc., and E. DIETZ, Engineer. Edited with Notes, by ROBERT MALLET, F.R.S., F.S.G., M.I.C.E., etc. American Edition, Edited with Notes and an Appendix on Iron Ores, by A. A. FESQUET, Chemist and Engineer. One volume, 12mo. $2.50

DUNCAN.—Practical Surveyor's Guide:
Containing the necessary information to make any person, of common capacity, a finished land surveyor without the aid of a teacher. By ANDREW DUNCAN. Illustrated. 12mo., cloth. .   .   . $1.25

DUPLAIS.—A Treatise on the Manufacture and Distillation of Alcoholic Liquors:
Comprising Accurate and Complete Details in Regard to Alcohol from Wine, Molasses, Beets, Grain, Rice, Potatoes, Sorghum, Asphodel, Fruits, etc.; with the Distillation and Rectification of Brandy, Whiskey, Rum, Gin, Swiss Absinthe, etc., the Preparation of Aromatic Waters, Volatile Oils or Essences, Sugars, Syrups, Aromatic Tinctures, Liqueurs, Cordial Wines, Effervescing Wines, etc., the Aging of Brandy and the Improvement of Spirits. with Copious Directions and Tables for Testing and Reducing Spirituous Liquors, etc., etc. Translated and Edited from the French of MM. DUPLAIS, Ainé et Jenne. By M. McKENNIE, M.D. To which are added the United States Internal Revenue Regulations for the Assessment and Collection of Taxes on Distilled Spirits. Illustrated by fourteen folding plates and several wood engravings. 743 pp., 8vo. $10.00

DUSSAUCE.—A General Treatise on the Manufacture of Every Description of Soap:
Comprising the Chemistry of the Art, with Remarks on Alkalies, Saponifiable Fatty Bodies, the apparatus necessary in a Soap Factory, Practical Instructions in the manufacture of the various kinds of Soap, the assay of Soaps, etc., etc. Edited from Notes of Larmé, Fontenelle, Malapayre, Dufour, and others, with large and important additions by Prof. H. DUSSAUCE, Chemist. Illustrated. In one vol., 8vo. . $10.00

DUSSAUCE.—A General Treatise on the Manufacture of Vinegar:

Theoretical and Practical. Comprising the various Methods, by the Slow and the Quick Processes, with Alcohol, Wine, Grain, Malt, Cider, Molasses, and Beets; as well as the Fabrication of Wood Vinegar, etc., etc. By Prof. H. DUSSAUCE. In one volume, 8vo. . . $5.00

DUSSAUCE.—A New and Complete Treatise on the Arts of Tanning, Currying, and Leather Dressing:

Comprising all the Discoveries and Improvements made in France, Great Britain, and the United States. Edited from Notes and Documents of Messrs. Sallerou, Grouvelle, Duval, Dessables, Labarraque, Payen, René, De Fontenelle, Malapeyre, etc., etc. By Prof. H. DUSSAUCE, Chemist. Illustrated by 212 wood engravings. 8vo. $25.00

DUSSAUCE.—A Practical Guide for the Perfumer:

Being a New Treatise on Perfumery, the most favorable to the Beauty without being injurious to the Health, comprising a Description of the substances used in Perfumery, the Formulæ of more than 1000 Preparations, such as Cosmetics, Perfumed Oils, Tooth Powders, Waters, Extracts, Tinctures, Infusions, Spirits, Vinaigres, Essential Oils, Pastels, Creams, Soaps, and many new Hygienic Products not hitherto described. Edited from Notes and Documents of Messrs. Debay, Lunel, etc. With additions by Prof. H. DUSSAUCE, Chemist. 12mo. $3.00

DUSSAUCE.—Practical Treatise on the Fabrication of Matches, Gun Cotton, and Fulminating Powders.

By Prof. H. DUSSAUCE. 12mo. $3.00

Dyer and Color-maker's Companion:

Containing upwards of 200 Receipts for making Colors, on the most approved principles, for all the various styles and fabrics now in existence; with the Scouring Process, and plain Directions for Preparing, Washing-off, and Finishing the Goods. In one vol., 12mo. . $1.25

EASTON.—A Practical Treatise on Street or Horse-power Railways.

By ALEXANDER EASTON, C.E. Illustrated by 23 plates. 8vo., cloth. $2.00

ELDER.—Questions of the Day:

Economic and Social. By Dr. WILLIAM ELDER. 8vo. . $3.00

FAIRBAIRN.—The Principles of Mechanism and Machinery of Transmission:

Comprising the Principles of Mechanism, Wheels, and Pulleys, Strength and Proportions of Shafts, Coupling of Shafts, and Engaging and Disengaging Gear. By Sir WILLIAM FAIRBAIRN, C.E., LL.D., F.R.S., F.G.S. Beautifully illustrated by over 150 wood-cuts. In one volume, 12mo. $2.50

FORSYTH.—Book of Designs for Headstones, Mural, and other Monuments:

Containing 78 Designs. By JAMES FORSYTH. With an Introduction by CHARLES BOUTELL, M.A. 4to., cloth. $5.00

GIBSON.—The American Dyer:

A Practical Treatise on the Coloring of Wool, Cotton, Yarn and Cloth, in three parts. Part First gives a descriptive account of the Dye Stuffs; if of vegetable origin, where produced, how cultivated, and how prepared for use; if chemical, their composition, specific gravities, and general adaptability, how adulterated, and how to detect the adulterations, etc. Part Second is devoted to the Coloring of Wool, giving recipes for one hundred and twenty-nine different colors or shades, and is supplied with sixty colored samples of Wool. Part Third is devoted to the Coloring of Raw Cotton or Cotton Waste, for mixing with Wool Colors in the Manufacture of all kinds of Fabrics, gives recipes for thirty-eight different colors or shades, and is supplied with twenty-four colored samples of Cotton Waste. Also, recipes for Coloring Beavers, Doeskins, and Flannels, with remarks upon Anilines, giving recipes for fifteen different colors or shades, and nine samples of Aniline Colors that will stand both the Fulling and Scouring process. Also, recipes for Aniline Colors on Cotton Thread, and recipes for Common Colors on Cotton Yarns. Embracing in all over two hundred recipes for Colors and Shades, and ninety-four samples of Colored Wool and Cotton Waste, etc. By RICHARD H. GIBSON, Practical Dyer and Chemist. In one volume, 8vo. .   . $12.50

GILBART.—History and Principles of Banking:

A Practical Treatise. By JAMES W. GILBART, late Manager of the London and Westminster Bank. With additions. In one volume, 8vo., 600 pages, sheep $5.00

Gothic Album for Cabinet Makers:

Comprising a Collection of Designs for Gothic Furniture. Illustrated by 23 large and beautifully engraved plates. Oblong .   . $3.00

GRANT. — Beet-root Sugar and Cultivation of the Beet.

By E. B. GRANT. 12mo. $1.25

GREGORY.—Mathematics for Practical Men :

Adapted to the Pursuits of Surveyors, Architects, Mechanics, and Civil Engineers. By OLINTHUS GREGORY. 8vo., plates, cloth $3.00

GRISWOLD.—Railroad Engineer's Pocket Companion for the Field :

Comprising Rules for Calculating Deflection Distances and Angles, Tangential Distances and Angles, and all Necessary Tables for Engineers ; also the art of Levelling from Preliminary Survey to the Construction of Railroads, intended Expressly for the Young Engineer, together with Numerous Valuable Rules and Examples. By W. GRISWOLD. 12mo., tucks $1.75

GRUNER.—Studies of Blast Furnace Phenomena.

By M. L. GRUNER, President of the General Council of Mines of France, and lately Professor of Metallurgy at the Ecole des Mines. Translated, with the Author's sanction, with an Appendix, by L. D. B. Gordon, F. R. S. E., F. G. S. Illustrated. 8vo. .   .   . $2.50

GUETTIER.—Metallic Alloys:

Being a Practical Guide to their Chemical and Physical Properties, their Preparation, Composition, and Uses. Translated from the French of A. GUETTIER, Engineer and Director of Foundries, author of "La Fouderie en France," etc., etc. By A. A. FESQUET, Chemist and Engineer. In one volume, 12mo. $3.00

HARRIS.—Gas Superintendent's Pocket Companion.

By HARRIS & BROTHER, Gas Meter Manufacturers, 1115 and 1117 Cherry Street, Philadelphia. Full bound in pocket-book form $2.00

Hats and Felting:

A Practical Treatise on their Manufacture. By a Practical Hatter. Illustrated by Drawings of Machinery, etc. 8vo. . . . $1.25

HOFMANN.—A Practical Treatise on the Manufacture of Paper in all its Branches.

By CARL HOFMANN. Late Superintendent of paper mills in Germany and the United States; recently manager of the Public Ledger Paper Mills, near Elkton, Md. Illustrated by 110 wood engravings, and five large folding plates. In one volume, 4to., cloth; 398 pages $15.00

HUGHES.—American Miller and Millwright's Assistant.

By WM. CARTER HUGHES. A new edition. In one vol., 12mo. $1.50

HURST.—A Hand-Book for Architectural Surveyors and others engaged in Building:

Containing Formulæ useful in Designing Builder's work, Table of Weights, of the materials used in Building, Memoranda connected with Builders' work, Mensuration, the Practice of Builders' Measurement, Contracts of Labor, Valuation of Property, Summary of the Practice in Dilapidation, etc., etc. By J. F. HURST, C.E. Second edition, pocket-book form, full bound $2.50

JERVIS.—Railway Property:

A Treatise on the Construction and Management of Railways; designed to afford useful knowledge, in the popular style, to the holders of this class of property; as well as Railway Managers, Officers, and Agents. By JOHN B. JERVIS, late Chief Engineer of the Hudson River Railroad, Croton Aqueduct, etc. In one vol., 12mo., cloth $2.00

JOHNSTON.—Instructions for the Analysis of Soils, Limestones, and Manures.

By J. F. W. JOHNSTON. 12mo. 38

KEENE.—A Hand-Book of Practical Gauging:
For the Use of Beginners, to which is added, A Chapter on Distillation, describing the process in operation at the Custom House for
ascertaining the strength of wines. By JAMES B. KEENE, of H. M.
Customs. 8vo. $1.25

**KELLEY.—Speeches, Addresses, and Letters on In-
dustrial and Financial Questions.**
By Hon. WILLIAM D. KELLEY, M. C. In one volume, 544 pages,
8vo. $3.00

KENTISH.—A Treatise on a Box of Instruments,
And the Slide Rule; with the Theory of Trigonometry and Loga-
rithms, including Practical Geometry, Surveying, Measuring of Tim-
ber, Cask and Malt Gauging, Heights, and Distances. By THOMAS
KENTISH. In one volume. 12mo. $1.25

KOBELL.—ERNI.—Mineralogy Simplified:
A short Method of Determining and Classifying Minerals, by means
of simple Chemical Experiments in the Wet Way. Translated from
the last German Edition of F. VON KOBELL, with an Introduction to
Blow-pipe Analysis and other additions. By HENRI ERNI, M. D.,
late Chief Chemist, Department of Agriculture, author of "Coal Oil
and Petroleum." In one volume, 12mo.   .   .   . $2.50

LANDRIN.—A Treatise on Steel:
Comprising its Theory, Metallurgy, Properties, Practical Working,
and Use. By M. H. C. LANDRIN, Jr., Civil Engineer. Translated
from the French, with Notes, by A. A. FESQUET, Chemist and Engineer. With an Appendix on the Bessemer and the Martin Processes
for Manufacturing Steel, from the Report of Abram S. Hewitt, United
States Commissioner to the Universal Exposition, Paris, 1867. In one
volume, 12mo. $3.00

**LARKIN.—The Practical Brass and Iron Founder's
Guide:**
A Concise Treatise on Brass Founding, Moulding, the Metals and their
Alloys, etc.: to which are added Recent Improvements in the Manu-
facture of Iron, Steel by the Bessemer Process, etc., etc. By JAMES
LARKIN, late Conductor of the Brass Foundry Department in Reany,
Neafie & Co's. Penn Works, Philadelphia. Fifth edition, revised,
with Extensive additions. In one volume, 12mo.   .   . $2.25

LEAVITT.—Facts about Peat as an Article of Fuel:
With Remarks upon its Origin and Composition, the Localities in
which it is found, the Methods of Preparation and Manufacture, and
the various Uses to which it is applicable; together with many other
matters of Practical and Scientific Interest. To which is added a chapter on the Utilization of Coal Dust with Peat for the Production of an
Excellent Fuel at Moderate Cost, specially adapted for Steam Service.
By T. H. LEAVITT. Third edition. 12mo.   .   .   . $1.75

LEROUX, C.—A Practical Treatise on the Manufactu1e of Worsteds and Carded Yarns:

Comprising Practical Mechanics, with Rules and Calculations applied to Spinning; Sorting, Cleaning, and Scouring Wools; the English and French methods of Combing, Drawing, and Spinning Worsteds and Manufacturing Carded Yarns. Translated from the French of CHARLES LEROUX, Mechanical Engineer, and Superintendent of a Spinning Mill, by HORATIO PAINE, M. D., and A. A. FESQUET, Chemist and Engineer. Illustrated by 12 large Plates. To which is added an Appendix, containing extracts from the Reports of the International Jury, and of the Artisans selected by the Committee appointed by the Council of the Society of Arts, London, on Woollen and Worsted Machinery and Fabrics, as exhibited in the Paris Universal Exposition, 1867. 8vo., cloth. $5.00

LESLIE (Miss).—Complete Cookery:

Directions for Cookery in its Various Branches. By MISS LESLIE. 60th thousand. Thoroughly revised, with the addition of New Receipts. In one volume, 12mo., cloth. $1.50

LESLIE (Miss).—Ladies' House Book:

A Manual of Domestic Economy. 20th revised edition. 12mo., cloth.

LESLIE (Miss).—Two Hundred Receipts in French Cookery.

Cloth, 12mo.

LIEBER.—Assayer's Guide:

Or, Practical Directions to Assayers, Miners, and Smelters, for the Tests and Assays, by Heat and by Wet Processes, for the Ores of all the principal Metals, of Gold and Silver Coins and Alloys, and of Coal, etc. By OSCAR M. LIEBER. 12mo., cloth. . . $1.25

LOTH.—The Practical Stair Builder:

A Complete Treatise on the Art of Building Stairs and Hand-Rails, Designed for Carpenters, Builders, and Stair-Builders. Illustrated with Thirty Original Plates. By C. EDWARD LOTH, Professional Stair-Builder. One large 4to. volume. $10.00

LOVE.—The Art of Dyeing, Cleaning, Scouring, and Finishing, on the Most Approved English and French Methods:

Being Practical Instructions in Dyeing Silks, Woollens, and Cottons, Feathers, Chips, Straw, etc. Scouring and Cleaning Bed and Window Curtains, Carpets, Rugs, etc. French and English Cleaning, any Color or Fabric of Silk, Satin, or Damask. By THOMAS LOVE, a Working Dyer and Scourer. Second American Edition, to which are added General Instructions for the Use of Aniline Colors. In one volume, 8vo., 343 pages. $5.00

MAIN and BROWN.—Questions on Subjects Connected with the Marine Steam-Engine:
And Examination Papers; with Hints for their Solution. By THOMAS J. MAIN, Professor of Mathematics, Royal Naval College, and THOMAS BROWN, Chief Engineer, R. N. 12mo., cloth. . . . $1.50

MAIN and BROWN.—The Indicator and Dynamometer:
With their Practical Applications to the Steam-Engine. By THOMAS J. MAIN, M. A. F. R., Assistant Professor Royal Naval College, Portsmouth, and THOMAS BROWN, Assoc. Inst. C. E., Chief Engineer, R. N., attached to the Royal Naval College. Illustrated. From the Fourth London Edition. 8vo. $1.50

MAIN and BROWN.—The Marine Steam-Engine.
By THOMAS J. MAIN, F. R.; Assistant S. Mathematical Professor at the Royal Naval College, Portsmouth, and THOMAS BROWN, Assoc. Inst. C. E., Chief Engineer R. N. Attached to the Royal Naval College. Authors of "Questions connected with the Marine Steam-Engine," and the "Indicator and Dynamometer." With numerous Illustrations. In one volume, 8vo. $5.00

MARTIN.—Screw-Cutting Tables, for the Use of Mechanical Engineers:
Showing the Proper Arrangement of Wheels for Cutting the Threads of Screws of any required Pitch; with a Table for Making the Universal Gas-Pipe Thread and Taps. By W. A. MARTIN, Engineer. 8vo. 50

Mechanics' (Amateur) Workshop:
A treatise containing plain and concise directions for the manipulation of Wood and Metals, including Casting, Forging, Brazing, Soldering, and Carpentry. By the author of the "Lathe and its Uses." Third edition. Illustrated. 8vo. $3.00

MOLESWORTH.—Pocket-Book of Useful Formulæ and Memoranda for Civil and Mechanical Engineers.
By GUILFORD L. MOLESWORTH, Member of the Institution of Civil Engineers, Chief Resident Engineer of the Ceylon Railway. Second American, from the Tenth London Edition. In one volume, full bound in pocket-book form. $2.00

NAPIER.—A System of Chemistry Applied to Dyeing.
By JAMES NAPIER, F. C. S. A New and Thoroughly Revised Edition. Completely brought up to the present state of the Science, including the Chemistry of Coal Tar Colors, by A. A. FESQUET, Chemist and Engineer. With an Appendix on Dyeing and Calico Printing, as shown at the Universal Exposition, Paris, 1867. Illustrated. In one volume, 8vo., 422 pages. $5.00

NAPIER.—Manual of Electro-Metallurgy:
Including the Application of the Art to Manufacturing Processes. By JAMES NAPIER. Fourth American; from the Fourth London edition, revised and enlarged. Illustrated by engravings. In one vol., 8vo. $2.00

NASON.—Table of Reactions for Qualitative Chemical Analysis.
By HENRY B. NASON, Professor of Chemistry in the Rensselaer Polytechnic Institute, Troy, New York. Illustrated by Colors.   .   63

NEWBERY.—Gleanings from Ornamental Art of every style:
Drawn from Examples in the British, South Kensington, Indian, Crystal Palace, and other Museums, the Exhibitions of 1851 and 1862, and the best English and Foreign works. In a series of one hundred exquisitely drawn Plates, containing many hundred examples. By ROBERT NEWBERY. 4to, ... $15.00

NICHOLSON.—A Manual of the Art of Bookbinding:
Containing full instructions in the different Branches of Forwarding, Gilding, and Finishing. Also, the Art of Marbling Book-edges and Paper. By JAMES B. NICHOLSON. Illustrated. 12mo., cloth. $2.25

NICHOLSON.—The Carpenter's New Guide:
A Complete Book of Lines for Carpenters and Joiners. By PETER NICHOLSON. The whole carefully and thoroughly revised by H. K. DAVIS, and containing numerous new and improved and original Designs for Roofs, Domes, etc. By SAMUEL SLOAN, Architect. Illustrated by 80 plates. 4to. $4.50

NORRIS.—A Hand-book for Locomotive Engineers and Machinists:
Comprising the Proportions and Calculations for Constructing Locomotives; Manner of Setting Valves; Tables of Squares, Cubes, Areas, etc., etc. By SEPTIMUS NORRIS, Civil and Mechanical Engineer. New edition. Illustrated. 12mo., cloth.   .   .   . $2.00

NYSTROM.—On Technological Education, and the Construction of Ships and Screw Propellers:
For Naval and Marine Engineers. By JOHN W. NYSTROM, late Acting Chief Engineer, U. S. N. Second edition, revised with additional matter. Illustrated by seven engravings. 12mo.   .   . $1.50

O'NEILL.—A Dictionary of Dyeing and Calico Printing:
Containing a brief account of all the Substances and Processes in use in the Art of Dyeing and Printing Textile Fabrics; with Practical Receipts and Scientific Information. By CHARLES O'NEILL, Analytical Chemist; Fellow of the Chemical Society of London; Member of the Literary and Philosophical Society of Manchester; Author of "Chemistry of Calico Printing and Dyeing." To which is added an Essay on Coal Tar Colors and their application to Dyeing and Calico Printing. By A. A. FESQUET, Chemist and Engineer. With an Appendix on Dyeing and Calico Printing, as shown at the Universal Exposition, Paris, 1867. In one volume, 8vo., 491 pages.   . $6.00

ORTON.—Underground Treasures:
How and Where to Find Them. A Key for the Ready Determination
of all the Useful Minerals within the United States. By JAMES
ORTON, A. M. Illustrated, 12mo. $1.50

OSBORN.—American Mines and Mining:
Theoretically and Practically Considered. By Prof. H. S. OSBORN.
Illustrated by numerous engravings. 8vo. (*In preparation.*)

OSBORN.—The Metallurgy of Iron and Steel:
Theoretical and Practical in all its Branches; with special reference
to American Materials and Processes. By H. S. OSBORN, LL. D.,
Professor of Mining and Metallurgy in Lafayette College, Easton,
Pennsylvania. Illustrated by numerous large folding plates and
wood-engravings. 8vo. $15.00

OVERMAN.—The Manufacture of Steel:
Containing the Practice and Principles of Working and Making Steel.
A Handbook for Blacksmiths and Workers in Steel and Iron, Wagon
Makers, Die Sinkers, Cutlers, and Manufacturers of Files and Hard-
ware, of Steel and Iron, and for Men of Science and Art. By FRED-
ERICK OVERMAN, Mining Engineer, Author of the "Manufacture of
Iron," etc. A new, enlarged, and revised Edition. By A. A. FESQUET,
Chemist and Engineer. $1.50

**OVERMAN.—The Moulder and Founder's Pocket
Guide:**
A Treatise on Moulding and Founding in Green-sand, Dry-sand, Loam,
and Cement; the Moulding of Machine Frames, Mill-gear, Hollow-
ware, Ornaments, Trinkets, Bells, and Statues; Description of Moulds
for Iron, Bronze, Brass, and other Metals; Plaster of Paris, Sulphur,
Wax, and other articles commonly used in Casting; the Construction
of Melting Furnaces, the Melting and Founding of Metals; the Composition of Alloys and their Nature. With an Appendix containing
Receipts for Alloys, Bronze, Varnishes and Colors for Castings; also,
Tables on the Strength and other qualities of Cast Metals. By FRED-
ERICK OVERMAN, Mining Engineer, Author of "The Manufacture
of Iron." With 42 Illustrations. 12mo. $1.50

Painter, Gilder, and Varnisher's Companion:
Containing Rules and Regulations in everything relating to the Arts
of Painting, Gilding, Varnishing, Glass-Staining, Graining, Marbling,
Sign-Writing, Gilding on Glass, and Coach Painting and Varnishing;
Tests for the Detection of Adulterations in Oils, Colors, etc.; and a
Statement of the Diseases to which Painters are peculiarly liable, with
the Simplest and Best Remedies. Sixteenth Edition. Revised, with
an Appendix. Containing Colors and Coloring – Theoretical and
Practical. Comprising descriptions of a great variety of Additional
Pigments, their Qualities and Uses, to which are added, Dryers, and
Modes and Operations of Painting, etc. Together with Chevreul's
Principles of Harmony and Contrast of Colors. 12mo., cloth. $1.50

PALLETT.—The Miller's, Millwright's, and Engineer's Guide.
By HENRY PALLETT. Illustrated. In one volume, 12mo. $3.00

PERCY.—The Manufacture of Russian Sheet-Iron.
By JOHN PERCY, M.D., F.R.S., Lecturer on Metallurgy at the Royal School of Mines, and to The Advanced Class of Artillery Officers at the Royal Artillery Institution, Woolwich ; Author of " Metallurgy." With Illustrations. 8vo., paper.   .   .   .   .   .   50 cts.

PERKINS.—Gas and Ventilation.
Practical Treatise on Gas and Ventilation. With Special Relation to Illuminating, Heating, and Cooking by Gas. Including Scientific Helps to Engineer-students and others. With Illustrated Diagrams. By E. E. PERKINS. 12mo., cloth. $1.25

PERKINS and STOWE.—A New Guide to the Sheet-iron and Boiler Plate Roller :
Containing a Series of Tables showing the Weight of Slabs and Piles to produce Boiler Plates, and of the Weight of Piles and the Sizes of Bars to produce Sheet-iron ; the Thickness of the Bar Gauge in decimals ; the Weight per foot, and the Thickness on the Bar or Wire Gauge of the fractional parts of an inch ; the Weight per sheet, and the Thickness on the Wire Gauge of Sheet-iron of various dimensions to weigh 112 lbs. per bundle ; and the conversion of Short Weight into Long Weight, and Long Weight into Short. Estimated and collected by G. H. PERKINS and J. G. STOWE. $2.50

PHILLIPS and DARLINGTON.—Records of Mining and Metallurgy ;
Or Facts and Memoranda for the use of the Mine Agent and Smelter. By J. ARTHUR PHILLIPS, Mining Engineer, Graduate of the Imperial School of Mines, France, etc., and JOHN DARLINGTON. Illustrated by numerous engravings. In one volume, 12mo.   .   . $2.00

PROTEAUX.—Practical Guide for the Manufacture of Paper and Boards.
By A. PROTEAUX, Civil Engineer, and Graduate of the School of Arts and Manufactures, and Director of Thiers' Paper Mill, Puy-de-Dôme. With additions, by L. S. LE NORMAND. Translated from the French, with Notes, by HORATIO PAINE, A.B., M.D. To which is added a Chapter on the Manufacture of Paper from Wood in the United States, by HENRY T. BROWN, of the "American Artisan." Illustrated by six plates, containing Drawings of Raw Materials, Machinery, Plans of Paper-Mills, etc., etc. 8vo. $10.00

REGNAULT.—Elements of Chemistry.
By M. V. REGNAULT. Translated from the French by T. FORREST BETTON, M.D., and edited, with Notes, by JAMES C. BOOTH, Melter and Refiner U. S. Mint, and WM. L. FABER, Metallurgist and Mining Engineer. Illustrated by nearly 700 wood engravings. Comprising nearly 1500 pages. In two volumes, 8vo., cloth.   .   .   . $7.50

REID.—A Practical Treatise on the Manufacture of Portland Cement :

By HENRY REID, C. E. To which is added a Translation of M. A. Lipowitz's Work, describing a New Method adopted in Germany for Manufacturing that Cement, by W. F. REID. Illustrated by plates and wood engravings. 8vo. $6.00

RIFFAULT, VERGNAUD, and TOUSSAINT.—A Practical Treatise on the Manufacture of Varnishes.

By M M. RIFFAULT, VERGNAUD, and TOUSSAINT. Revised and Edited by M. F. MALEPEYRE and Dr. EMIL WINCKLER. Illustrated. In one volume, 8vo. (*In preparation*.)

RIFFAULT, VERGNAUD, and TOUSSAINT.—A Practical Treatise on the Manufacture of Colors for Painting :

Containing the best Formulæ and the Processes the Newest and in most General Use. By M M. RIFFAULT, VERGNAUD, and TOUSSAINT. Revised and Edited by M. F. MALEPEYRE and Dr. EMIL WINCKLER. Translated from the French by A. A. FESQUET, Chemist and Engineer. Illustrated by Engravings. In one volume, 650 pages, 8vo.
$7.50

ROBINSON.—Explosions of Steam Boilers :

How they are Caused, and how they may be Prevented. By J. R. ROBINSON, Steam Engineer. 12mo. $1.25

ROPER.—A Catechism of High Pressure or Non-Condensing Steam-Engines :

Including the Modelling, Constructing, Running, and Management of Steam Engines and Steam Boilers. With Illustrations. By STEPHEN ROPER, Engineer. Full bound tucks . . . $2.00

ROSELEUR.—Galvanoplastic Manipulations :

A Practical Guide for the Gold and Silver Electro-plater and the Galvanoplastic Operator. Translated from the French of ALFRED ROSELEUR, Chemist, Professor of the Galvanoplastic Art, Manufacturer of Chemicals, Gold and Silver Electro-plater. By A. A. FESQUET, Chemist and Engineer. Illustrated by over 127 Engravings on wood. 8vo., 495 pages. $6.00

☞ *This Treatise is the fullest and by far the best on this subject ever published in the United States.*

SCHINZ.—Researches on the Action of the Blast Furnace.

By CHARLES SCHINZ. Translated from the German with the special permission of the Author by WILLIAM H. MAW and MORITZ MULLER. With an Appendix written by the Author expressly for this edition. Illustrated by seven plates, containing 28 figures. In one volume, 12mo. $4.25

SHAW.—Civil Architecture:

Being a Complete Theoretical and Practical System of Building, containing the Fundamental Principles of the Art. By EDWARD SHAW, Architect. To which is added a Treatise on Gothic Architecture, etc. By THOMAS W. SILLOWAY and GEORGE M. HARDING, Architects. The whole illustrated by One Hundred and Two quarto plates finely engraved on copper. Eleventh Edition. 4to., cloth. . $10.00

SHUNK.—A Practical Treatise on Railway Curves and Location, for Young Engineers.

By WILLIAM F. SHUNK, Civil Engineer. 12mo. . . $2.00

SLOAN.—American Houses:

A variety of Original Designs for Rural Buildings. Illustrated by 26 colored Engravings, with Descriptive References. By SAMUEL SLOAN, Architect, author of the "Model Architect," etc., etc. 8vo. $2.50

SMEATON.—Builder's Pocket Companion:

Containing the Elements of Building, Surveying, and Architecture; with Practical Rules and Instructions connected with the subject. By A. C. SMEATON, Civil Engineer, etc. In one volume, 12mo. $1.50

SMITH.—A Manual of Political Economy.

By E. PESHINE SMITH. A new Edition, to which is added a full Index. 12mo., cloth. . . . . ·$1.25

SMITH.—Parks and Pleasure Grounds:

Or Practical Notes on Country Residences, Villas, Public Parks, and Gardens. By CHARLES H. J. SMITH, Landscape Gardener and Garden Architect, etc., etc. 12mo. $2.25

SMITH.—The Dyer's Instructor:

Comprising Practical Instructions in the Art of Dyeing Silk, Cotton, Wool, and Worsted, and Woollen Goods: containing nearly 800 Receipts. To which is added a Treatise on the Art of Padding; and the Printing of Silk Warps, Skeins, and Handkerchiefs, and the various Mordants and Colors for the different styles of such work. By DAVID SMITH, Pattern Dyer. 12mo., cloth. . . . $3.00

SMITH.—The Practical Dyer's Guide:

Comprising Practical Instructions in the Dyeing of Shot Cobourgs, Silk Striped Orleans, Colored Orleans from Black Warps, Ditto from White Warps, Colored Cobourgs from White Warps, Merinos, Yarns, Woollen Cloths, etc. Containing nearly 300 Receipts, to most of which a Dyed Pattern is annexed. Also, A Treatise on the Art of Padding. By DAVID SMITH. In one volume, 8vo. Price. . . $25.00

STEWART.—The American System.

Speeches on the Tariff Question, and on Internal Improvements, principally delivered in the House of Representatives of the United States. By ANDREW STEWART, late M. C. from Pennsylvania. With a Portrait, and a Biographical Sketch. In one volume, 8vo., 407 pages. $3.00

STOKES.—Cabinet-maker's and Upholsterer's Companion:
Comprising the Rudiments and Principles of Cabinet-making and Upholstery, with Familiar Instructions, illustrated by Examples for attaining a Proficiency in the Art of Drawing, as applicable to Cabinet-work; the Processes of Veneering, Inlaying, and Buhl-work; the Art of Dyeing and Staining Wood, Bone, Tortoise Shell, etc. Directions for Lackering, Japanning, and Varnishing; to make French Polish; to prepare the Best Glues, Cements, and Compositions, and a number of Receipts particularly useful for workmen generally. By J. STOKES. In one volume, 12mo. With Illustrations. . $1.25

Strength and other Properties of Metals:
Reports of Experiments on the Strength and other Properties of Metals for Cannon. With a Description of the Machines for testing Metals, and of the Classification of Cannon in service. By Officers of the Ordnance Department U. S. Army. By authority of the Secretary of War. Illustrated by 25 large steel plates. In one volume, 4to. . $10.00

SULLIVAN.—Protection to Native Industry.
By Sir EDWARD SULLIVAN, Baronet, author of "Ten Chapters on Social Reforms." In one volume, 8vo. $1.50

Tables Showing the Weight of Round, Square, and Flat Bar Iron, Steel, etc.,
By Measurement. Cloth. 63

TAYLOR.—Statistics of Coal:
Including Mineral Bituminous Substances employed in Arts and Manufactures; with their Geographical, Geological, and Commercial Distribution and Amount of Production and Consumption on the American Continent. With Incidental Statistics of the Iron Manufacture. By R. C. TAYLOR. Second edition, revised by S. S. HALDEMAN. Illustrated by five Maps and many wood engravings. 8vo., cloth. $10.00

TEMPLETON.—The Practical Examinator on Steam and the Steam-Engine:
With Instructive References relative thereto, arranged for the Use of Engineers, Students, and others. By WM. TEMPLETON, Engineer. 12mo. $1.25

THOMAS.—The Modern Practice of Photography.
By R. W. THOMAS, F. C. S. 8vo., cloth. 75

THOMSON.—Freight Charges Calculator.
By ANDREW THOMSON, Freight Agent. 24mo. . . . $1.25

TURNING: Specimens of Fancy Turning Executed on the Hand or Foot Lathe:
With Geometric, Oval, and Eccentric Chucks, and Elliptical Cutting Frame. By an Amateur. Illustrated by 30 exquisite Photographs. 4to. $3.00

Turner's (The) Companion:
Containing Instructions in Concentric, Elliptic, and Eccentric Turning; also various Plates of Chucks, Tools, and Instruments; and Directions for using the Eccentric Cutter, Drill, Vertical Cutter, and Circular Rest; with Patterns and Instructions for working them. A new edition in one volume, 12mo. $1.50

URBIN.—BRULL.—A Practical Guide for Puddling Iron and Steel.
By ED. URBIN, Engineer of Arts and Manufactures. A Prize Essay read before the Association of Engineers, Graduate of the School of Mines, of Liege, Belgium, at the Meeting of 1865-6. To which is added A COMPARISON OF THE RESISTING PROPERTIES OF IRON AND STEEL. By A. BRULL. Translated from the French by A. A. FESQUET, Chemist and Engineer. In one volume, 8vo. $1.00

VAILE.—Galvanized Iron Cornice-Worker's Manual:
Containing Instructions in Laying out the Different Mitres, and Making Patterns for all kinds of Plain and Circular Work. Also, Tables of Weights, Areas and Circumferences of Circles, and other Matter calculated to Benefit the Trade. By CHARLES A. VAILE, Superintendent "Richmond Cornice Works," Richmond, Indiana. Illustrated by 21 Plates. In one volume, 4to. $5.00

VILLE.—The School of Chemical Manures:
Or, Elementary Principles in the Use of Fertilizing Agents. From the French of M. GEORGE VILLE, by A. A. FESQUET, Chemist and Engineer. With Illustrations. In one volume, 12 mo.   .   . $1.25

VOGDES.—The Architect's and Builder's Pocket Companion and Price Book:
Consisting of a Short but Comprehensive Epitome of Decimals, Duodecimals, Geometry and Mensuration; with Tables of U. S. Measures, Sizes, Weights, Strengths, etc., of Iron, Wood, Stone, and various other Materials, Quantities of Materials in Given Sizes, and Dimensions of Wood, Brick, and Stone; and a full and complete Bill of Prices for Carpenter's Work; also, Rules for Computing and Valuing Brick and Brick Work, Stone Work, Painting, Plastering, etc. By FRANK W. VOGDES, Architect. Illustrated. Full bound in pocket-book form. $2.00
Bound in cloth. 1.50

WARN.—The Sheet-Metal Worker's Instructor:
For Zinc, Sheet-Iron, Copper, and Tin-Plate Workers, etc. Containing a selection of Geometrical Problems; also, Practical and Simple Rules for describing the various Patterns required in the different branches of the above Trades. By REUBEN H. WARN, Practical Tin-plate Worker. To which is added an Appendix, containing Instructions for Boiler Making, Mensuration of Surfaces and Solids, Rules for Calculating the Weights of different Figures of Iron and Steel, Tables of the Weights of Iron, Steel, etc. Illustrated by 32 Plates and 37 Wood Engravings. 8vo. $3.00

WARNER.—New Theorems, Tables, and Diagrams for the Computation of Earth-Work:

Designed for the use of Engineers in Preliminary and Final Estimates, of Students in Engineering, and of Contractors and other non-professional Computers. In Two Parts, with an Appendix. Part I.—A Practical Treatise ; Part II.—A Theoretical Treatise ; and the Appendix. Containing Notes to the Rules and Examples of Part I. ; Explanations of the Construction of Scales, Tables, and Diagrams, and a Treatise upon Equivalent Square Bases and Equivalent Level Heights. The whole illustrated by numerous original Engravings, comprising Explanatory Cuts for Definitions and Problems, Stereometric Scales and Diagrams, and a Series of Lithographic Drawings from Models, showing all the Combinations of Solid Forms which occur in Railroad Excavations and Embankments. By JOHN WARNER, A. M., Mining and Mechanical Engineer. 8vo. $5.00

WATSON.—A Manual of the Hand-Lathe:

Comprising Concise Directions for working Metals of all kinds, Ivory, Bone and Precious Woods ; Dyeing, Coloring, and French Polishing ; Inlaying by Veneers, and various methods practised to produce Elaborate work with Dispatch, and at Small Expense. By EGBERT P. WATSON, late of "The Scientific American," Author of "The Modern Practice of American Machinists and Engineers." Illustrated by 78 Engravings. $1.50

WATSON.—The Modern Practice of American Machinists and Engineers:

Including the Construction, Application, and Use of Drills, Lathe Tools, Cutters for Boring Cylinders, and Hollow Work Generally, with the most Economical Speed for the same ; the Results verified by Actual Practice at the Lathe, the Vice, and on the Floor. Together with Workshop Management, Economy of Manufacture, the Steam-Engine, Boilers, Gears, Belting, etc., etc. By EGBERT P. WATSON, late of the "Scientific American." Illustrated by 86 Engravings. In one volume, 12mo. $2.50

WATSON.—The Theory and Practice of the Art of Weaving by Hand and Power:

With Calculations and Tables for the use of those connected with the Trade. By JOHN WATSON, Manufacturer and Practical Machine Maker. Illustrated by large Drawings of the best Power Looms. 8vo. $10.00

WEATHERLY.—Treatise on the Art of Boiling Sugar, Crystallizing, Lozenge-making, Comfits, Gum Goods.

12mo. $2.00

WEDDING.—The Metallurgy of Iron;

Theoretically and Practically Considered. By Dr. HERMANN WEDDING, Professor of the Metallurgy of Iron at the Royal Mining Academy, Berlin. Translated by JULIUS DU MONT, Bethlehem, Pa. Illustrated by 207 Engravings on Wood, and three Plates. In one volume, 8vo. (In press.)

WILL.—Tables for Qualitative Chemical Analysis.
By Professor HEINRICH WILL, of Giessen, Germany. Seventh edition. Translated by CHARLES F. HIMES, Ph. D., Professor of Natural Science, Dickinson College, Carlisle, Pa.   .   .   . $1.50

WILLIAMS.—On Heat and Steam:
Embracing New Views of Vaporization, Condensation, and Explosions. By CHARLES WYE WILLIAMS, A. I. C. E.   Illustrated.   8vo. $3.50

WOHLER.—A Hand-Book of Mineral Analysis.
By F. WOHLER, Professor of Chemistry in the University of Göttingen.   Edited by HENRY B. NASON, Professor of Chemistry in the Rensselaer Polytechnic Institute, Troy, New York.   Illustrated.   In one volume, 12mo. $3 00

WORSSAM.—On Mechanical Saws:
From the Transactions of the Society of Engineers, 1869.   By S. W. WORSSAM, Jr.   Illustrated by 18 large plates.   8vo.   .   . $5.00

www.ingramcontent.com/pod-product-compliance
Lightning Source LLC
Chambersburg PA
CBHW030905270326
41929CB00008B/590